"Chad Bird has done it again: written a soul-stirring guide to grace in everyday life, brimming with heart, insight, and poetry. Along the way, he inverts the expectations that creep into our heads, pointing to the comfort and freedom of the gospel. I am so grateful for his voice and ministry."

David Zahl, director of Mockingbird Ministries and author of *Seculosity: How Career, Parenting, Technology, Food, Politics, and Romance Became Our New Religion*

"Chad Bird has not just set the value of success on its head but has restored to success its true meaning. Using vivid and vividly written examples, Chad demonstrates that success before God—success for Christians, in other words—operates through the collapse of worldly success. One wants to say, 'Say it isn't so, Chad!' But it is. And Chad proves it—delightfully, biblically, touchingly. *Upside-Down Spirituality* is really right-side-up."

Paul F. M. Zahl, retired Episcopal minister and theologian who identifies with Chad Bird's description of the Christian life

UPSIDE-DOWN
SPIRITUALITY

THE 9 ESSENTIAL FAILURES
OF A FAITHFUL LIFE

CHAD BIRD

BakerBooks
a division of Baker Publishing Group
Grand Rapids, Michigan

Published by Baker Books
a division of Baker Publishing Group
PO Box 6287, Grand Rapids, MI 49516-6287
www.bakerbooks.com

Printed in the United States of America

Library of Congress Cataloging-in-Publication Data
Names: Bird, Chad, author.
Title: Upside-down spirituality : the 9 essential failures of a faithful life / Chad Bird.
Description: Grand Rapids, MI : Baker Books, a division of Baker Publishing
    Group, [2019] | Includes bibliographical references.
Identifiers: LCCN 2018034275 | ISBN 9780801075674 (pbk.)
Subjects: LCSH: Christian life.
Classification: LCC BV4501.3 .B4958 2019 | DDC 248.4—dc23
LC record available at https://lccn.loc.gov/2018034275

19 20 21 22 23 24 25   7 6 5 4 3 2 1

To Carson and Jeanette,
my beloved parents

Contents

Introduction

Turning Our World Upside Down

A couple of miles from downtown San Antonio, nestled near some of the city's oldest neighborhoods, sits a quaint little home with blue siding and white colonnades. Inside are books that number in the thousands. They stand at attention on shelves that ascend from floor to vaulted ceiling. Others rest haphazardly atop one another on the faded green carpet. There are cheap paperback romances with browning pages, thick philosophical tomes, colorful travel journals. The rooms in which children once played, couples dreamed their dreams, and families broke bread together now shelter everyone from Aristotle to Dostoevsky. The musty smell of wisdom and antiquity paints the air.

To some it's just an old used bookstore, but to me it's a temple of humanity's ever-searching mind, seeking to capture some of this world's truth, beauty, and mystery in ink on paper.

The last time I visited this store, I pulled random books off the shelves, riffled through their pages. From one of them a slip of paper fell, fluttering to the floor like a bird with a broken wing. I stooped to pick it up. In my hand was a single faded and yellowed sheet, folded in half and dated June 9, 1999. It had camped out in that book for almost twenty years. I unfolded it and scanned the words. Two short but weighty questions were scribbled on it. I read them, then read them again, more slowly. I smiled, refolded the sheet of paper, and reunited it with the book that had been its protector. Someone else would discover the note. Someone else would read it. Perhaps the same questions were bouncing around in their own heads. At one time or another, I suppose we all ask them.

Nearly two decades ago our anonymous friend asked: "Does it matter what one believes? Or is anything okay, just so long as you feel good about it?"

What I'd give to sit down with our friend and inquire if, in the last twenty years, he or she has moved any closer to answering those questions. I was twenty-nine years old when that note was penned. I read it on the eve of my forty-seventh birthday. My own journey over those years has taken a myriad of unexpected twists and turns—and more set-backs than I care to remember. At the age of twenty-nine, I had life pretty well mapped out, the body of truth dissected and labeled, and the world divided into neat little black-and-white boxes. I was a pastor and, in two years, would become a professor. I would have demolished those two questions with well-honed arguments and a barrage of biblical proof-texts—perhaps with a dash of disdain in my voice.

Today, I'd likely say, "Hey, let's grab a beer and talk about it."

In that conversation—as in this one you and I are just beginning—I'd attempt to gently dig beneath those ground-level questions, to probe into some other matters. We could discuss what it means to be human, to be able to ask questions like that in the first place. We could talk about what believing is, what it means for something to matter, and how reliable (or not) our feelings are when it comes to truth. And because I believe there is a God, and that God actually loves us and wants to do good things for us, I'd try to steer the conversation toward that One who is truth itself.

Perhaps by then our glasses would be empty and we'd need to order another round. But that's okay. Drinks are on me.

Somewhere along our conversation, however, I'd endeavor to draw us down from whatever intellectual heights to which we may have soared, plant our feet on terra firma once more, and talk about truth not in the abstract but in the flesh. Touchable truth. Truth with hair and blood and fingernails. Along with crucifixion scars. Because if we never get around to talking about him—about the Truth named Jesus—then we're just a couple of beer-drinking amateur philosophers whiling away the hours on a Friday night. But if he becomes our subject, if that sacred and scarred embodiment of truth inhabits our minds, then we will have arrived at the answer to those questions tucked away in the folds of a book twenty years ago.

The one who is the Way, the Truth, and the Life—he and he alone can tell you what really matters. And he'll tell that if you believe in him, if you follow his call to be a disciple, it might not feel good—sometimes it'll hurt like hell—but it's the only path worth walking because you'll have as your companion the God who'll turn your life upside down in the best and craziest of ways.

Turning the World Upside Down

The early followers of Jesus had many false accusations lobbed at them. The emperor Nero blamed them for the fire that swept through Rome in AD 64. The Roman writer Tacitus claimed they practiced abominations and hated the human race. Early in the second century, the imperial legate Pliny wrote to Emperor Trajan that Christians held "a perverse and extravagant superstition." Because they refused to acknowledge the existence of Roman and Greek gods, they were labeled as atheists. Various adversaries even circulated outrageous lies that they "engaged in orgiastic sex, incest, and cannibalism."[1] Today we might call it a smear campaign spread by means of fake news.

But there was one accusation hurled against Christians that was much closer to the truth: their opponents in Thessalonica claimed these Jesus followers had "turned the world upside down" (Acts 17:6). Now they were on to something. What they didn't realize was that the God these Christians worshiped was himself the chief culprit. He took our globe in his hands, flipped it over, and gave it a mighty shake. Age-old foundations quivered and detached from the ground of human confidence. Corpses popped out of their graves like corks from bottles of champagne. Prostitutes and lepers tumbled into castles and kings sank down into the mire of the streets. God was engaged in his favorite pastime: upsetting our every expectation of how a respectable, dignified divinity should conduct himself. He was indeed turning everything upside down.

Nothing has changed since that first-century shake-up of the world. God has never remained, like a part-time repairman, waiting on our phone call when something needs fixing. When

he invades our lives, he kick-starts a long process of decon-
struction and reconstruction. C. S. Lewis pictured it this way:

> Imagine yourself as a living house. God comes in to rebuild that
> house. At first, perhaps, you can understand what he is doing.
> He is getting the drains right and stopping the leaks in the roof
> and so on: you knew that those jobs needed doing and so you
> are not surprised. But presently he starts knocking the house
> about in a way that hurts abominably and does not seem to
> make sense. What on earth is He up to? The explanation is that
> he is building quite a different house from the one you thought
> of—throwing out a new wing here, putting on an extra floor
> there, running up towers, making courtyards. You thought you
> were going to be made into a decent little cottage: but He is
> building a palace. He intends to come and live in it Himself.[2]

When Jesus "starts knocking the house about in a way
that hurts abominably," when his work in our lives "does
not seem to make sense," then he's really getting somewhere.
He's pounding gaping holes in the painted drywall of our own
wisdom to reveal the termite-infested 2x4s on the other side.
Ripping up the carpet to point out an inch-wide crack in the
foundation. What we thought would take a few months to fix
and fancy up will, it turns out, require a lifetime of labor. But
Christ is okay with that. He was, after all, raised in the home
of a carpenter. And he'll take his sweet time. C. S. Lewis says
he "intends to come and live in it Himself," but the truth is, he's
already moved in, put his underwear and socks in the drawers,
and buckled on his tool belt. He's here for the long haul.

The work of Jesus for us and in us does not seem to make
sense because it's not designed to. It's non-sense. What Paul

calls "the foolishness of God" (1 Cor. 1:25). His backward wisdom will earn him a big, fat F in Professor World's philosophy class. Jesus won't even correctly fill in the blanks to the most elementary questions.

Question: How do you save your life?

God: By losing it.

Question: Who are the greatest?

God: The forgotten, the anonymous, the least.

Question: How do you get ahead?

God: By putting everyone else first.

Jesus doesn't just color outside the lines. He turns the paper over and draws a brand-new image. His way of thinking (and reforming our minds), his way of acting (and redirecting our deeds), and his way of speaking (and reteaching our tongues) is so foreign to us that in virtually every situation in which he touches our lives, our first reaction will be to offer a prayer to him to reverse the very thing he's doing.

God's wisdom and ways seem so ungodlike not because they actually are but because they don't fit our preconceptions of how a divinity should act and where he should be. Our hearts, by nature and by nurture, hunt for him in all the wrong places. We lock our eyes on the heavens while all the while he's camped down at our feet. We look for him in success while he's waiting for us in failure.

It's bad enough that we are born with hearts that are "deceitful above all things" (Jer. 17:9). Worse yet, those same hearts are daily deceived even more. We're duped by a cacophony of cultural voices that go on and on with pretty little lies about God that we already want to believe because these falsehoods feed our egos. The secular spiritualists and religious self-helpers of our culture would have us believe in a God who believes in us. Half cheerleader, half life coach, this "Jesus" is all about our self-fulfillment and self-accomplishment, with personal happiness as our true salvation. Disney and Hollywood, far from simply offering entertainment, advertise a view of human nature that exalts pleasure as the highest good and being normal and average as a colossal embarrassment, and often treat religion in general—and Christianity in particular—as a ball and chain restraining us from a self-determined, carefree existence of chasing our dreams. From the moment we scroll through Facebook over coffee in the morning till we watch our favorite Netflix drama at night, we're being exposed to a barrage of messages about human nature, what's important in the world, and God's place in our lives. The messages are rarely explicit. They're embedded in the narratives, the advertisements, and the heroes and heroines of Hollywood. But their sway over people's perceptions—*our* perceptions—cannot be overestimated. The habits of our hearts are usually formed when we're unaware it's happening.

If our hearts are already deceived while we're in diapers, and if 99 percent of the cultural narratives about God are a bunch of religious malarkey, it's no great shock that when Jesus shows up on our doorstep we usually slam the door in his face. He's not selling what we want to buy. In fact, he's not selling anything. He's giving things away. Jesus has already footed the bill for us. He's here to give us life. To hand us hope. To enrich us with wisdom. The problem is that all his life and hope and wisdom just don't seem kosher to us. It's not what we think we want. Nor is it even what we think God would want for us.

So Jesus has his work cut out for him. He's going to have to turn our own little worlds upside down. Good thing he actually enjoys that. God takes pleasure in revamping our hearts and recalibrating the compass of our souls. It's what he does best. His life-changing, hope-giving, wisdom-bestowing love in action.

Jesus told us to pray to our Father, "Thy will be done," for a vital reason. His will and our will are usually on opposite ends of a tug-of-war rope, with a messy mud puddle between us. He's pulling us toward the very things we think are ludicrous, beneath us, unfulfilling, and painful. We're pulling him toward what we think—and what our society tells us—will make us feel important, satisfied, proud, and happy.

Thus, God's greatest doings for us will often seem, at the time, like our undoing. And in many ways, that's precisely what they are. He's tugging us through the mud puddle. He is undoing us, unconfusing us, undeceiving us. Just as the cross must come before Easter arrives, so in Christ we must die "to the elemental spirits of the world" (Col. 2:20), its assumptions and pseudowisdom, that we might arise with new eyes illumined by the Spirit. And these new eyes that see things from a divine perspective will point our feet down paths that lead to the blessed achievement of failure.

Achieving Failure

George Foreman grew up with a stomach starved for food and a heart fattened with anger. Ashamed of revealing his poverty in the cafeteria, he'd carry a brown paper lunch bag to school. It was empty. He gave vent to his rage through his fists, first in the streets and later in the boxing ring. Opponent after opponent crumbled to the mat as six-foot-four Foreman rose through the ranks undefeated. This giant with an iron fist seemed unstoppable.

In 1974, legendary Muhammad Ali challenged Foreman to a championship match. All bets were on Foreman, who, at twenty-five, was seven years younger than Ali. Round after round, Ali took all that Foreman could dish out. Punch after punch landed but Ali remained on his feet, even taunting his opponent. Foreman gradually weakened. In the eighth round, Ali hit him with a lightning fast right hand that sent Foreman tumbling. He stumbled back to his feet at the count of nine but the judges wouldn't let the fight continue. Ali was declared the winner. And Foreman swallowed the bitter pill of defeat for the first time.

Three years later, in Puerto Rico, he reentered the ring to face another fighter, Jimmy Young. If he won this match, he'd have a chance to go after Ali again and retrieve his title. The two pounded away at each other, but neither gained the upper hand. Until the ninth round. Foreman took a blow that knocked him to his knees. He managed to get up but it was all over. In the end, once more, the judges put his opponent on top. Foreman had failed again, only this time the pain was far deeper.

After the fight, in his dressing room, Foreman paced the floor, still in a daze. He thought he was going to die. He said he "could literally smell death in the room." He began to pray that God would spare his life. Suddenly, he collapsed, feeling like he was in a "deep, dark junkyard of nothing." Moments later, prostrate on a table, he said to himself, "I don't care if this is death. I still believe there's a God." No sooner had he said that when "a gigantic hand reached in and held" him. He "jumped off the table and started screaming, 'Jesus Christ has come alive in me! . . . I got to save the world!'" Foreman said, "That experience changed me forever."[3]

Those two failures, and the near-death experience after the second one, were watershed moments for Foreman. He walked away from his boxing career. In time he would become a pastor and devote time and resources to helping young people. Looking back, he said it was like his whole biography had "been turned upside down." The successes he'd enjoyed early in his career he now considered the real failure because he didn't appreciate them.

Foreman's experience of failure ruined him in the best possible way. It spoiled his vision of what he considered the good life. Pre-failure, his ambition was fueled by the desire for conquest, victory, looking down at the opponent he had overcome. The goal of his life was to be extraordinary, a champion. In other words, Foreman's view of the good life was a life all about him. His desires. His dreams. His will being done. Not until he swallowed that bitter pill of defeat did he begin to taste the sweet hope of something radically new, something better. As much as it hurt, as much as it was contrary to everything Foreman wanted, failure was God's gift to him.

When God sends the gift of failure to us, we often take a magic marker and write on the package, "Return to sender!" Thanks, but no thanks. We don't want it. Obviously, the Lord mailed it to the wrong person. It's for that loser down the street who never mows his lawn and whose dogs bark all night. There's no way this is for us. I mean, it's not only what we don't want. It's also not what we've asked God for and prayed to receive. So he shows up on our front porch to hand it to us himself. *Yes, this is for you.*

Failures, big and small, are God's ways of prying open our eyes to see what we'd never see otherwise. Had Foreman gone on undefeated, winning every fight, he'd always have had a skewed image of what life is really all about. God uses singular failures to get us off the path we're on and back on the path he himself walks—the path where he continues to turn our world upside down.

On that path we begin to learn something strange. We come to grips with just how weird Christianity is, how un-cool and unmainstream it is. Because from the perspective of the world, from the view of common sense, Jesus and his followers are an embarrassing band of failures. We fail to believe that life is all about us. We fail to follow our hearts. We fail to have the kind of marriages and be the kinds of parents the world thinks we should be. We even fail to be the kind of church that is socially acceptable and religiously smart according to common human standards. On God's path we learn, often the hard way, that anytime the world stands to its feet and applauds what we're doing, there's a high likelihood we're doing it all wrong. But to fail the world—that is to achieve the upside-down spiritual life.

The Good Life

If you really want to dig down to the core of what someone believes, what drives them in everything, from relationships, to careers, to where they choose to live, and often to whom they vote for, ask them, What do you consider to be the good life?

It's one of those questions that all of us answer, whether consciously or unconsciously (usually the latter). We entertain a particular vision in our minds, an orientation of our hearts, toward what we think will be good for us. What we deem a life worth living. We may or may not actually be living that life. It might be—and often is—simply a daydream. But it's still there, pushing us in certain directions, shaping our decisions, and playing a huge role in our emotional and spiritual well-being.

For many the good life is a life full of good things: a nice home, sizable savings, plenty of toys, the newest gadgets. It's characterized by acquisition and consumption, getting and enjoying those possessions that they think will ultimately make their hearts smile. For others, the good life is defined in terms of accomplishments. When I finish my degree, when I land that promotion, when I win that trophy, when I lose those pounds, when I reach retirement, then I'll finally be living the good life. For still others, it's all about how others see them or treat them. The good life happens when people finally accept me for who I am, when my parents are proud of me, when my wife looks up to me, when my husband begins to show me affection, when people don't see me as ugly or fat or disabled or poor or depressed. For them, the good life is entirely reflected in the eyes of others. *Their* estimation of *my* worth and acceptability.

And we could go on. Everyone has some set of criteria by which they define a life worth living. A good life. A blessed life.

Rarely, however, will you cross paths with someone who says the good life starts by dying. Dying would be the end of the good life, right? For believers, no. It's the only possible genesis of it. Without first undergoing death, there is no chance of living the good life our Lord desires for us. God's good life begins with our death.

Consider how abnormal this is. In almost every situation, when we want to effect change within us, what do we do? We begin with what we already have and build on that. If I'm tipping the scale at 350 pounds and climbing a single flight of stairs leaves me red-faced, I can buy a gym membership and hire a trainer. She'll get me spinning on a treadmill, pumping iron, and insist on more salads and less chocolate cake. Over time, I can sweat off the pounds, build muscle mass, and improve my breathing. My trainer begins with my body, unhealthy as it is, and whips it into shape. Or if I lack education, I can enroll in college, camp out at the library, and attend conferences. Gradually, I'll accumulate knowledge, raise my IQ, beef up my vocabulary. I'll strengthen the mind I already have. Whether I want to cultivate positive change in my health, marriage, finances, work performance, or public speaking, I'll work with what I have. With enough time, effort, expense, and commitment, I can become the better businessperson, spouse, athlete, or student I want to be. The way forward begins with where I already am.

And then there's God's mode of operation. When Jesus gets his hands on us, he throws everything into reverse. He doesn't begin where we already are. He doesn't work with what we've got. He doesn't size us up, diagnose our strengths and weaknesses, and implement a program of self-improvement. In fact, what we deem our strengths are, in his estimation, often graver problems than our weaknesses because they breed confidence in ourselves.

Instead, Christ always goes for the nuclear option: he kills us. Or, to put it more precisely, he kills us by pulling us up onto the cross with him. We co-die with Jesus. Co-bleed with him. Are co-buried and then co-resurrected with him. God is not in the business of making us better; he's on a mission to make us dead. Dead on the cross with Jesus to everything that defines us as frail, flawed, prideful humans. Dead with Jesus to our misplaced aspirations, our selfish dreams, our egocentric universe. Co-crucifixion with Jesus is the genesis of the good life. Because before we can truly live, we must first truly die to the un-life, the non-life, we once had apart from him.

The good life is thus a Good Friday kind of life. On that day God himself turned the world upside down by transforming what looked like failure into the victory of salvation for all. While everyone gawked and jeered at that bloody, naked, executed criminal, labeling him a total loser, God knew what he was doing. He chose to exhibit his wisdom under the guise of foolishness. He was reigning over a kingdom that unaided human eyes saw—and will always see—as a colossal flop.

And into this foolish failure of a kingdom he carries us within his body, even as he himself resides within our bodies. "It is no longer I who live," the Christian says, "but Christ who lives in me" (Gal. 2:20), for I have already journeyed from death to resurrection in him. It is no longer I who work and play, but Christ who works and plays in me. It is no longer I who love and believe, but Christ who loves and believes in me. It is no longer I who am a husband and father, wife and mother, police officer or teacher, pastor or pilot, but Christ who is all these in me. Our union with Christ by virtue of our co-death and co-resurrection with him now defines us. It is who we are. It is how our Father sees us. And it is how the Spirit enables us to see ourselves.

If we are so inextricably united with such a misunderstood savior, then we'll be misunderstood disciples. Many, if not most, will think our confession of the good life makes no sense. In fact, though they might never say it to our face, they'll think our life choices are quite stupid, backward, and even insulting. And I don't mean merely the talking heads who champion secular ideologies but coworkers, neighbors, and those who share our last names. Early in his ministry, Jesus's own family thought he had gone off the deep end. They tried to grab him and force him to come home since he was evidently "out of his mind" (Mark 3:21). The religious bigwigs upped the ante by accusing Jesus of housing a demon in his head. "He is possessed by Beelzebul," they claimed (v. 22).

To follow Jesus, in other words, is often a lonely way. It is never the path chosen by the majority. But Christ never claimed it was. "Enter by the narrow gate," he said. "For the gate is wide and the way is easy that leads to destruction, and those who enter by it are many. For the gate is narrow and the way is hard that leads to life, and those who find it are few" (Matt. 7:13–14).

But through the narrow gate and in that hard way we find Life. Life with a capital *L*. We find the one who is "the way, and the truth, and the life" (John 14:6). Or, rather, he finds us. He searches us out, lifts us up, and carries us into his Father's kingdom. Indeed, so narrow is the gate leading to life that there's only room for one person to squeeze through—Jesus. The only way we get in is astraddle his shoulders. As the shepherd carried the lost lamb home on his shoulders, rejoicing the whole way, so Jesus smiles and laughs his way back to the Father with us slung around his neck. He brings us home. He rescues us from the carnivals of triviality in which we're wasting our time on dead-end dreams. He frees us from the maze of monetary acquisition that impoverishes our souls. He liberates us from the slavery to emotionalism, radical individualism, and various versions of the egocentric American dream. And he reveals a better way, the only good way. A way that actually accords with being human—with being a son or daughter of God, a brother and sister to all other people, an earthly creature who also bears the image and likeness of the Creator. In Jesus our worlds are turned upside down. But we find, to our utter amazement, that upside down in him is actually right side up. What we thought was death before is actually life, and what we thought was life was death. What we deemed undesirable failures before are successes, and what we deemed successes are, in reality, failures.

Failures of a faithful life—that's what we'll be talking about in the chapters to follow. What this world's common-sense wisdom reckons as failures, anyway. The failure to be extraordinary, the failure to live independent lives, the failure to go big or go home, the failure to think love sustains our marriages, even the failure to have a personal relationship with Jesus. George Foreman said that his whole biography had "been turned upside down." So it will be with us. If not our whole biography, then at least a few chapters of it. For there are areas in all our lives—personally, in our families and marriages, as well as in our churches—where we've become so habituated to the empty platitudes of our culture that we don't even realize our hearts have gone astray.

The early Christians were accused of turning the world upside down. The greatest compliment we can receive is the accusation that we are doing the same. When that happens, we'll know the truth: that the Spirit is rebuilding us through his Word to be, think, believe, and act as free people, liberated by the death and resurrection of Jesus into the good life of those beloved by God.

PART 1
OURSELVES

1

The Good News That God Doesn't Believe in You

The Failure to Believe in Ourselves

Stuck to the dashboard of my Freightliner truck is a small, rectangular calendar, no bigger than 3x4 inches. The top part advertises a fertilizer company that is one of my customers, a regular stop on my delivery route. Beneath the company's name, logo, and address are the dozen sheets of paper that document my progress from January to December. One of my daily rituals, before I kill the diesel engine and clock out, is to take my pen and X out the day just completed. Then, at the close of each month, I rip off that sheet, crumple it up, and toss it in the trash. Time marches on.

At the beginning of the year, that little calendar is in pristine shape. The top part candy-apple red, the twelve sheets of paper cotton white, their edges razor straight. But by the time "Joy to the World" dances through the speakers, that calendar looks utterly joyless. Used up. Worn out. Smudges of dirt and grease from my fingers mar the colors. One corner is peeled up where the sticky back came unglued. The edges of December's page are torn and bent and haggard.

The year is not kind to the calendar. As all too often it is not kind to us.

Remember that January? The one that, like a seed swaddled in fertile soil, appeared full of potential, primed for growth and fruitfulness? It would be a good year, maybe even a great year, you thought. Your kids were healthy. Your marriage solid. Your job secure. Then, one by one, the ensuing months not only mocked your optimism but tested and—at times—seemed to erode your faith.

Last year was like that for my sister, Rayna. In January, she scanned the months ahead and smiled to herself. She and her husband, Scott, were both healthy. They had one beautiful little granddaughter from their son, and had just found out, around the Christmas tree, that their oldest daughter would bless them with another grandchild in early October. Like that pristine calendar, the year looked bright and shiny, packed with potential.

Then a gloomy May dragged itself onto her doorstep. While redoing her bathroom, Rayna missed a step down from the ladder, fell, and almost blacked out from the pain. She would spend the summer healing from a broken leg. Scott, a farmer and rancher, would be sick for weeks in the fall, barely able to leave the house to care for his cattle and crops.

But these monthly trials were child's play compared to August. Their daughter went into labor early and little Remington Faith ("Remi") entered all our lives—a full eight weeks before her due date. Due to heart issues and serious breathing difficulties, Remi would spend the rest of that year in the NICU, on a ventilator.

While that year held many blessings, including the birth of this granddaughter, the journey from January to December also left the family worn out, their faith tested, and—like my dashboard calendar—feeling more haggard than healthy.

That was my sister's year. But I bet you have your own. The Year of Great Expectations that became the Year of Cancer, the Year of Divorce, the Year of Bankruptcy, the Year of Funerals. Or maybe it was no single dramatic event. Just an exhaustingly long series of little things that all added up to a year that left you feeling washed up, struggling to hope, and craving a fresh start.

Fresh starts are what January 1 is all about, especially after a year stained with disappointments. 'Tis the season of New Year's resolutions. The floodgates of social media will spill forth with inspirational memes: "What lies behind us and what lies before us are tiny matters compared to what lies within us."[1] Or, "Believe in yourself and the rest will fall into place. Have faith in your own abilities, work hard, and there is nothing you cannot accomplish."[2] They all strike a similar chord: within you is limitless potential, if you only believe it, tap into it, make it your own. This year can be the best of years if you'll believe the best about yourself, that you possess the wherewithal to make it happen.

But, if these New Year sentiments still taste a little bland, like they need a dash of religion sprinkled on top, you can also see quotes along the lines of, "God never gives you more than you can handle. You've got this." Or, "No mountain is too high, no ocean is too vast, no dream is too grand, if you'll trust that God has trust in you." Oftentimes these words from the movie *Elmer Gantry* will be quoted to prop up the downtrodden and urge them to drink deeply of the potential bottled up in January 1: "You may not believe in God, but God believes in you."

On the cusp of a new year, especially after twelve months of setbacks and face-plants, these positive proverbs of human potential and divine reinforcement can raise our flagging spirits and buoy our sinking hopes. They can be the secret to success as we take our next steps forward into an uncertain future.

Or they can be the most disastrous advice we've ever received.

To know which, we need to ask ourselves some fundamental questions, beginning with a very simple one: Is it possible that your bad year is, from God's perspective, the year in which he did his best work in you? Is what we label bad often what God calls good?

We begin to find the answer to those questions in the rise and fall of a famous Babylonian king.

The King Enthroned in Dirt

Nebuchadnezzar was living the Babylonian dream. He had become the man, the myth, the legend. Everything a guy might desire in his wildest imagination was already his in spades: unlimited power, immeasurable wealth, prestige, honor, accolades, women, you name it. If he so desired, he could have breakfast in bed, hunt big game that afternoon, wine and dine his friends that evening, and sate his sexual appetite between the sheets of the harem that night. He possessed what many men would kill for. To say that he was enjoying the good life is the understatement of the century. Nebuchadnezzar was a rock star, business mogul, international celebrity, and playboy—all rolled into one.

And he was doomed.

One night Nebuchadnezzar had a dream that everything he treasured would one day be trashed. He would be driven away from other people to live like an animal—chewing on grass, drenched by dew, having the mind of a beast (Dan. 4:1–26). Daniel, who interpreted the dream, warned him to repent, to show mercy to the poor, to do righteousness (v. 27). But the king was deaf to his plea.

At first, it seemed this strange dream had been just a passing nightmare, not a prophetic warning. After all, for the next twelve months nothing changed. His life was still smooth sailing. He was living the plush lifestyle of the rich and famous.

Then one day, while strolling atop his royal palace, he scanned his grandiose metropolis and let his ego do the talking: "Is not this the great Babylon I have built as the royal residence, by my mighty power and for the glory of my majesty?" (v. 30 NIV). No sooner did the words leave the king's mouth when that nightmarish dream finally did come true.

In the aftermath, Nebuchadnezzar's "good life" was revealed for what it really was—vanity of vanities, a sand castle washed away by the rising tides of divine judgment.

This ruler entered the worst years of his life, which turned out to be the best years of his life. "Best" not because they were full of smiles or suffering-free or prosperous. They were terrible. It's a weird scene, but picture the king growing hair long like eagle feathers and fingernails like the claws of a bird, crawling on all fours as he chewed on grass like a cow its cud (v. 33). The man was utterly undone. He lost everything. A debased, despicable, frightening caricature of a human being. No biblical figure plummeted more deeply into an animalistic, subhuman existence than did this once smug, narcissistic king.

And yet it was here, in the low of lows, that he was finally reconciled to the High of Highs. At the close of his suffering, he raised his eyes toward heaven and his sanity was restored. He praised the Most High, honoring and glorifying him who lives forever (v. 34). Eventually his nobles sought him out, and he was raised from the dirt back to the throne. The closing verse of his narrative is telling: "Now I, Nebuchadnezzar, praise and exalt and glorify the King of heaven, because everything he does is right and all his ways are just. And those who walk in pride he is able to humble" (v. 37 NIV).

"Those who walk in pride he is able to humble." Before his worst year, the king would not, *could* not, have uttered this best confession. To put it in New Testament terms, God crucified Nebuchadnezzar. He put this proud man to death in order that he might give Nebuchadnezzar new and true life. The king lost himself in order that he might find, in his emptiness, the God who alone could fill that void within him. This complete failure of a man discovered, wrapped within that failure, the kind of heavenly success that only Christ can give.

This story illustrates, in graphic detail, that what we label as bad the Lord often knows is good for us. This is how the Lord of the cross works. We look at life through glory-eyes but he looks at our lives through cross-eyes. Where we see death, he sees life. Where we see loss, he sees gain. He does indeed turn everything upside down.

And what he did for Nebuchadnezzar in a big way, he also does for us in smaller ways. We might not be swaggering atop our palaces, chests puffed out as we relish our world-renowned accomplishments, but we all lug about our pride, our trophies, our self-sufficiency, our addiction to control, our insatiable egos. And they all have a divine bull's-eye on them. Because the Father loves us, he disciplines us and humbles us (Heb. 12:6). In that God-given humility, and only there, do we become more aware of the fact that sometimes the worst years of our lives are those years when God is doing some of his best work within us.

The Nebuchadnezzar Syndrome

Our lifelong struggle is what we might call the Nebuchadnezzar Syndrome. Like the king, we are natural-born believers. It's just that we always gravitate toward believing the wrong thing. We perform quite well at putting our faith in everything but God. And there's a vast smorgasbord of options. Life is like a cafeteria. Grab your tray and amble along, spooning a little power onto your plate, using tongs to lift some wealth, slicing off a big piece of control. Wash it all down with a sugar-soaked, super-sized glass of self-esteem. Our palates are all unique, and the god options are virtually limitless, so each of us winds up with a tray heaped full of diverse divinities that we think will assuage our spiritual appetite.

What we discover, as the king did long ago, is that what looks appetizing, what tastes sweet, what goes down smooth, is usually poison masquerading as a meal.

Christ runs a very different kind of kitchen. And even though the courses he serves and the drinks he pours are manifold, all of them are nothing but various ways he puts himself inside us and us inside himself.

The Breastplate of St. Patrick sums up the menu in the kitchen of Jesus:

> Christ with me,
> Christ before me,
> Christ behind me,
> Christ in me,
> Christ beneath me,
> Christ above me,
> Christ on my right,
> Christ on my left,
> Christ when I lie down,
> Christ when I sit down,
> Christ when I arise,
> Christ in the heart of every man who thinks of me,
> Christ in the mouth of everyone who speaks of me,
> Christ in every eye that sees me,
> Christ in every ear that hears me.[3]

Ireland's patron saint is poetically extending what Paul wrote to the Philippians: "For to me to live is Christ, and to die is gain" (1:21). In an old hymn we give triple emphasis to this truth: "Jesus, Jesus, only Jesus, can my heartfelt longing still."[4]

Christ alone. Jesus, Jesus, only Jesus. He is the sole meal of the Father. The bread that comes down from heaven to give life to the world (John 6:51). The exclusive food and drink who nourishes us as nothing and no one else can, for he is the flesh-and-blood embodiment of the Father's love.

The Nebuchadnezzar Syndrome is like a spiritual eating disorder. It channels our appetites in a multitude of directions but never toward Christ. It seduces us into believing that our peace, our fulfillment, our purpose are found in a life where we get what we want. Where all our dreams come true. Where we believe in ourselves. And where even God believes in us. In other words, this syndrome bids us pursue a life in which everything revolves around us. Our desires become the touchstone of what is good or bad.

There Is a Way That Seems Right

"There is a way that seems right to a man, but its end is the way to death" (Prov. 16:25). Wise old Solomon wrote these words. And if there's anyone who would know the truth of them, he's the man.

In one of his other books, Ecclesiastes, Solomon documents his own quest for the good life. He sought for it in wisdom, in cramming his brain full of facts and discoveries and wonders. "He spoke of trees, from the cedar that is in Lebanon to the hyssop that grows out of the wall. He spoke also of beasts, and of birds, and of reptiles, and of fish" (1 Kings 4:33). He "was wiser than all other men" (v. 31). Yet he concluded that "in much wisdom is much vexation, and he who increases knowledge increases sorrow" (Eccles. 1:18).

He also sought the good life in pleasure, in laughter, in wine, in architecture, in gardening, in lovers, in the acquisition of servants and animals and precious objects (2:1–9). "Whatever my eyes desired," he wrote, "I did not keep from them. I kept my heart from no pleasure" (v. 10).

His conclusion? "All was vanity and a striving after wind" (v. 11). King Solomon, like his Babylonian counterpart, possessed everything a person might desire, including an IQ that was out of this world, yet in the end he realized he was a fool. No better than an imbecile sprinting after the breeze on a hot summer day.

"There is a way that seems right to a man, but its end is the way to death" (Prov. 16:25). The Hebrew word for "way" is *derek*, which refers not only to a path or road but a way of life. A vision of what constitutes human happiness and fulfillment. More than a lifestyle, it's a mind-style, a heart-style, a way of being human in this world. Solomon realized the *derek* he was on, racing after intelligence, pleasure, and wealth as the goals of life, led to only one place—a deep, yawning pit of destruction. It may seem right, it may feel good, but the euphoria is temporary. Ocean water may, at the moment, quench the thirst of a man floating at sea, but in a few hours he'll be dead. So it is with many *dereks* that people travel in this life.

What *derek*, which way, are you on? How do you envision what it means to be human in this world? You may not be Solomon, but you've probably conducted your own experiments. Some search for the good life in the intellectual rigors of the academic world. Others seek it in a string of sexual hookups. Others pore over every self-help book they can find. Some look for it by immersing themselves in work, in the collection of expensive toys, in sculpting their bodies at the gym, in boasting the biggest bank account among their friends. We're all looking for that "one thing" that will make us feel worthy, important, like our lives are not a waste.

Here's a little secret, though: all these ways—the innumerable bad ones and the singular good one—lead to death. The only question is whether this death will be the end of our life or the genesis of true, abundant life.

"I have come that they may have life," Jesus said, "and have it to the full" (John 10:10 NIV). This life Jesus speaks of, this overflowing life, always has its origin in emptiness. The emptiness our friend Nebuchadnezzar experienced when he toppled from the throne to the dirt. The emptiness that Solomon discovered when all his wine and women and brainpower turned out to be a dead-end street. And it's the emptiness to which Christ leads all of us when we realize that *we* are the problem—not the solution—to our lives.

This unwelcome truth cannot be stressed enough. The ultimate problem is not that we lack self-esteem but that we are engrossed in ourselves. The problem is not that we don't believe in ourselves, or believe that God believes in us, but that we've set ourselves up as the object of faith. We arrive in this world with the assumption that we are the center of it. Good comes to be defined by what pleases us, satisfies us, entertains us, makes us feel better about who we are. We aren't born with clean slates, as it were, with the whiteboard of our hearts just waiting for words to be written upon it. The words are already there. Rather, a word is already there, scribbled over and over—the word *me, me, me,* repeated a thousand times. The solution to life, the way we achieve true joy and contentment, cannot be found within ourselves because we are the problem.

What we need is failure. Failure to believe in ourselves. Failure to believe that God believes in us. A Nebuchadnezzar kind of failure, in which our eyes are unglued from our navel and directed outward to the only one who can transform this death of self into a resurrection into life.

God's New Year's Resolution for Us

Rather than asking what our New Year's resolution might be, let's ask what God's resolution for us is—what his good and gracious will is for our lives. It turns out to be the same on January 1 as on March 1 and July 1, all the way to December 31. God's resolution is simply this: *to get us out of ourselves and into his Son.*

Rather than encouraging us to believe in ourselves, the Spirit gives us faith to trust in the Lord who remains faithful, even "if we are faithless . . . for he cannot deny himself" (2 Tim. 2:13). Rather than telling us to look within and tap into our potential, he's hard at work "fixing our eyes on Jesus, the pioneer and perfecter of faith" (Heb. 12:2 NIV).

In his novel *The Hammer of God*, Bo Giertz tells the story of Fridfeldt, a young pastor in Sweden who is passionate about obedience, holy living, producing spiritual fruits, being that person who always has his religious ducks in a row.[5] On the surface, anyway, Fridfeldt seems to be the poster boy of discipleship. But his weakness is precisely that seeming strength.

Every hour of every day, this man's resolution is focused in a singular direction: on himself. Yes, it's a focus on doing holy stuff, but that is all smoke and mirrors. Fridfeldt, intensely religious though he may be, is really no different than a secularist. His eyes are on his works, his heart, his activity, his achievements. He is the center of his religious world. His "Jesus" is not so much a savior of sinners as a cheerleader of doers.

One Sunday, the Spirit finally begins to have his way with this young pastor. It's Transfiguration, the day when the church celebrates Jesus's revelation of glory to Peter, James, and John atop the mountain (Matt. 17:1–8). Fridfeldt grabs a little book of sermons and steps into the pulpit to read one of them. One verse from the Bible story catches his eye as he scans the page. It's near the end of the Gospel account, after Moses and Elijah disappear, after the Father speaks, after the cloud that enveloped Jesus vanishes. Speaking of the disciples, it says, "And when they lifted up their eyes, they saw no one but Jesus only" (v. 8).

Looking out over the congregation, Fridfeldt begins to read the sermon aloud. As he does, he realizes, with a growing astonishment, that no one needs to hear this sermon more than he does. The old pastor who had authored this little collection of homilies had been reposing in the parish cemetery for the last half-century, but on this momentous day, he stood in the pulpit, as it were, alongside Fridfeldt, proclaiming a message about "Jesus only."

"The law constrains a man to look chiefly at himself," Fridfeldt reads. Indeed, it does. Like a mirror, it constantly throws our flawed perfection back at us. And not only the "big-L" Laws like the Ten Commandments but the "little-l" laws as well.[6] "Little-l" laws are "the demands we feel every day from our culture, those around us, or ourselves."[7] Like the laws that command, "Thou shalt be skinny," "Thou shalt be successful," "Thou shalt believe in thyself," or "Thou shalt always come in first place." The high and holy day of "little-l" laws is New Year's day, when we resolve to fix ourselves, improve ourselves, make ourselves right. All these laws push us in only one direction: back to ourselves, inside ourselves, not to Christ.

As Fridfeldt continues to preach, the words of this old sermon begin to awaken in him an upside-down understanding of discipleship. In the mess of his life, he has lost sight of Jesus. He has been running "the endless way of the law." A steep pathway "bordered by naked trees whose supple branches hung down like whips." The way of the law, the pathway of obedience and perfection and self-centered spirituality "lies endlessly before you, bringing continually severer demands and constantly growing indebtedness." But "suddenly Christ stood there in the middle of the road. Now his old thoughts gave way to something new and wonderful: Jesus only, righteousness for each and every one who believed. The pathway had an end!"[8] That end is Christ, who is "the end of the law" (Rom. 10:4).

"Jesus only," the sermon accentuated over and over, like "hammer blows aimed with unerring precision against the head of a nail."[9] Jesus only is The End of the endless road of self-improvement, self-salvation, self-belief—the me-me-me trinity of the ego's religion. Jesus only is our conversion. Jesus only is our justification. Jesus only is our sanctification.

Like the disciples atop the mountain on the day of our Lord's transfiguration, we lift up our eyes to see no one save Jesus. No hope save Jesus. No peace save Jesus. We become monomaniacs about Christ. He's the only one who rescues us from a vain life of pursuing false gods. The only one who meets us in our death to fill us with abundant life.

If we are our problem, then Jesus and Jesus alone is our solution.

What the Spirit revealed to Fridfeldt that day in the pulpit, he reveals to each of us as we stand at our desks, in our kitchens, in our classrooms: life is not about us. It's not about how strong or weak we are, how smart or dumb we are, how flabby or fit we are. It's not about believing in ourselves or God believing in us. Life is all about losing our flawed and egocentric identities in a co-death with Christ and being raised to newness of life in his resurrection.

One of the best gifts we can receive is the failure to put trust in ourselves. One of the most important truths to learn is that God doesn't believe in us. He is the one who is trustworthy. He doesn't believe in us; he does something profoundly better: he loves us. Our Father doesn't peer within us, pinpoint some hidden quality worthy of his affection and trust, and then act on that discovery.

Before we were born, before we were either bad or good, dependable or undependable, lovable or unlovable—from all eternity our Father loved us. He didn't go on a hunt to find people deserving of his grace. Quite the contrary!

> You see, at just the right time, when we were still powerless, Christ died for the ungodly. Very rarely will anyone die for a righteous person, though for a good person someone might possibly dare to die. But God demonstrates his own love for us in this: While we were still sinners, Christ died for us. (Rom. 5:6–8 NIV)

Grab hold of these words: "When we were still powerless . . . while we were still sinners." Robert F. Capon reminds us that "if the Gospel is about anything, it is about the God who meets us where we are, not where we ought to be— 'while we were still sinners.'"[10] The gospel is "not some self-improvement scheme devised by a God who holds back on us till he sees the improvements. Above all, Jesus wants to make sure we understand that he doesn't care a fig about our precious results. It doesn't even make a difference to him if we're solid brass bastards, because 'while we were still sinners, Christ died for the ungodly.'"[11]

Jesus knows good and well that there's nothing inside us worth believing in. In fact, everything inside us looks absolutely untrustworthy. If anything, when the Lord peers into our hearts, he should hightail it for the hills, getting as far away from us as he can. But he's not that kind of God. He loves before he looks. And even after he looks, he still loves. Because his love has nothing to do with us. It is not sparked by our goodness or sustained by our obedience. God is love. It's who he is and what he does. While we were still powerless, he was powerful to save. While we were still sinners, he was still the sinless, gracious, saving God he's always been.

Our life as husbands and wives, moms and dads, teachers and truck drivers is a Jesus-only life. Whether we have a smiles-and-laughter year or a dumpster-fire year; whether we are at the top of our game or hunkering down in the shadows of defeat; whether we completed an Iron Man or were so depressed we just binge-watched Netflix, every day of that year is lived in Christ alone. When the Father sees us, he sees his Son. Period. Full stop. He doesn't see a glowing success or an embarrassing failure, he sees Jesus. "You have died, and your life is hidden with Christ in God" (Col. 3:3). And there's no safer hiding place in the world than there.

In Jesus only do we become the people we were created to be. The Father's children. His holy family. There is the good life, for we become part of the body of the good and gracious Savior. Every "thou shalt" ends in him. He is the end of little-l laws and big-L laws. When we are in Jesus, no law

44

can accuse us any more than it can accuse Christ. Here is the freedom found in being loved—unconditionally, unceasingly, by the God whose grace covers every single flaw we have.

In Jesus only we fail to believe in the pseudo-god who believes in us. Instead, we believe in the God who is crazy over us. Who can't lavish enough love upon us. Who is head-over-heels for his children. Gone is all this ego-talk of self-this and self-that. Here to stay is the Jesus-talk of forgiveness, mercy, new creation, and abundant life.

The good news for all of us who, like Nebuchadnezzar, lose ourselves and find God in failure is that God will never lose us. Never fail us. Instead, he'll keep right on rejoicing over us, laughing in love over the children who mean more to him than anything else in heaven and earth.

Blessed are those who fail to believe in themselves, who fail to believe that God believes in them, for they shall find in Jesus-only everything their heart desires.

2

What If I Just Want to Be Average?

The Failure to Make a Name for Ourselves

John was born in the land of Mardi Gras and the hometown of jazz. The year was 1937. I suppose every mother, as she rocks her baby to sleep, daydreams of what the child in her arms will grow up to be. But John's mother harbored zero doubts about one thing: her son would grow up to be Somebody. His father was a mechanic, and she gave private music lessons at their home, but this boy from New Orleans would be anything but average. He would make a name for himself.

And he did, at an early age. John's high IQ enabled him to skip right over first grade. When he was ten years old, he was involved in stage productions, emceed a children's radio show, and did some modeling. Opportunities abounded for this precocious child. Later, in his teenage years, he honed his writing skills. At the age when most kids were happy simply to earn their driver's license, sixteen-year-old John was not only editing the school newspaper and winning essay contests but also typing away at his first novel. It seemed his mother's intuition was spot-on. John was anything but a run-of-the-mill young man.

His crowning achievement was not long in coming. While serving in the military, then upon returning home to care for his ailing father, John was crafting his masterpiece: another novel that he hoped would rock the literary world. And that it did. Most authors have to labor in obscurity for years, if not decades, before they stand a chance at recognition, let alone fame. But John was only in his twenties when he put the final touches on the manuscript that would lead to international acclaim. In the first year of its publication, fifty thousand copies flew off the shelves. The book would go on to win the highest award conceivable for a writer—the Pulitzer Prize. This classic American novel has been translated into eighteen languages, and over two million copies are now in print. John accomplished the extraordinary. His mother had been right. He made a name for himself. He rose to the top. He became Somebody.

Only John never knew any of this. His novel, *A Confederacy of Dunces*, initially attracted the interest of a few publishers but was eventually rejected by them all. The pile of typewritten pages, his masterpiece, collected dust atop a dresser in his bedroom, a mocking emblem of unfulfilled aspirations. Waves of disappointment and depression crashed over him. He finally gave up hope altogether. On March 26, 1969, he drove to Biloxi, Mississippi, parked his car, and ran a garden hose from the exhaust into the car window. John Kennedy Toole was thirty-one years old.

Eleven years after John's suicide, the novel was finally published, thanks to the indefatigable efforts of his mother. This son of a blue-collar laborer, the boy from New Orleans, did indeed become Somebody. He was worlds away from mediocre. But he discovered, far too early and far too fatally, that a flaming passion for fame and notoriety is also a bonfire that can consume and destroy.

What the Hell Is Water?

This flaming passion, this drive to outdo others, was kindled in the heart of John by his mother. And that's how it begins to glow inside many of us. If not our mothers, our fathers light the fire. If not our parents, our teachers. And if not our teachers or coaches or mentors, then we pick up the spark from the innumerable fires of ambition that burn on our cultural landscape. Be somebody. Stand out from the crowd. Rise above your peers. Carve out a name for yourself. Be anything but normal. These desires are as American as apple pie. They are orthodox exclamations in the national creed.

The hit song "Only in America," by the country music duo Brooks and Dunn, sounds the beat of this dance of ambition. It was played at George W. Bush's inauguration party in 2001, at the Democratic National Convention in 2004, and after Barak Obama's acceptance speech in 2008. In the opening lines, a bus driver in New York City scans the faces of the children in his rearview mirror. What does he see? One kid who takes a job to help his family make ends meet. Another kid who'll end up incarcerated. But also one who "just might be president." Because in America, as the chorus boasts, "we dream as big as we want to."[1]

Yes, we do. In fact, to question the validity of this aspiration is tantamount to heresy. Of course, we want our children to dream as big as they want to. Of course, we want them to rise to the top, achieve the extraordinary, scale the ladder of success. To suggest otherwise is to undermine the very ethos of a country that boasts that it's the place where you can be anything you want to be.

And yet, to question the accepted, assumed validity of the world's fundamental aspirations is part of the daily vocation of the follower of Jesus. "Do not be conformed to this world," Paul writes, "but be transformed by the renewal of your mind, that by testing you may discern what is the will of God, what is good and acceptable and perfect" (Rom. 12:2). We can't avoid conforming to the world unless we constantly ask what the world believes—and whether it is what Christ would have us believe and follow.

David Foster Wallace, in his 2005 commencement speech at Kenyon College, provides us with a parable to think about this discernment and awareness:

> There are these two young fish swimming along, and they happen to meet an older fish swimming the other way, who nods at them and says, "Morning, boys. How's the water?" And the two young fish swim on for a bit, and then eventually one of them looks over at the other and goes, "What the hell is water?"[2]

The cultural waters in which we swim are so natural, so ever-present, so much a part of the fixed reality of our lives, that we rarely pause to ponder, "What the hell is water?" What are these wet assumptions soaking our skin? What are these "truths" that form the sea in which we live and work and play? Awareness of the core beliefs of our culture, and an interrogation of their validity, is the kind of hard work we dare not shirk. And part of that interrogative work is questioning what place—if any—the quest to be extraordinary should have in our lives.

The Beginner's Guide to Giving Your Sin a Holy Name

Down the block from my childhood home in Jal, New Mexico, was a magical place, spilling over with amazing machines of every shape and size. Here the music of invention and restoration echoed throughout the day. The odors of muscle and speed and raw energy wafted through the air. Sure, to unimaginative adults it was just another dirty mechanic's shop where you could get mufflers installed and carburetors tuned. But to me, it was the holy playground of boyhood, where tools and grease and fuel—the sacraments of manhood—were on full display. This yard of iron was a holy site to which I made a weekly pilgrimage.

The "No Trespassing" signs only made it more irresistible.

I guess you could say I suffered from an overly active imagination as a child. Perhaps that partly explains why one day, upon finding a ring of keys in my dad's desk drawer, I decided that one of these keys would surely fit one of the many cars and trucks strewn about the mechanic's yard. So I pocketed them. My six-year-old brain had yet to plot a thorough plan of action. But I had the first three steps down: (1) My buddy Tom and I would sneak into the mechanic's yard. (2) We'd match key and car together. (3) We'd sit inside the car.

Who knows what we would have done next. As it turns out, we got no further than the first step.

"What are you boys doing?" I was crouching on greasy soil beside a red 1974 Chevrolet pickup when the words were bellowed from behind me. Tom and I had been trying every key on my dad's keychain, but all in vain. None would open the driver's side door. As I slowly pivoted my head to the voice, I looked up, first from her widespread feet, then on to her pillar-like legs, up to arms crossed over a massive bosom, and finally to her face. There stood the mechanic's wife, her lips locked in a snarl.

It seemed to me that Tom and I had three viable options at this critical juncture. One, we could bolt for the alley and high-tail it to the relative safety of my backyard. Two, we could spill the beans and beg for clemency from the giantess. Or, three, I could take the lead and try to lie my way out of this jam.

Of course, I chose the third option.

Having only a few years of truth-twisting experience under my belt, I was still pretty much a novice. But I did the best I could under the circumstances. "Well, we," I stammered, jerking a thumb in Tom's direction, "my friend and I, were gonna, you know, we were gonna. . ."

"You were gonna what?" she spat.

"We were gonna fix this truck," I finally managed to say.

She just stared at us. Her face didn't soften. Seconds passed. Things were falling apart quickly. As if communicating telepathically, Tom and I knew what we had to do. Since option three had not panned out, we reverted to option one. As if on cue, we both bolted for the alley.

Martin Luther once said that sin never wants to be sin; it always wants to be righteousness.[3] Although I was too young to have mastered the skill of lying, I also knew there was no way I was telling this woman the truth. Confessing was not a real option. Why? I didn't want this to be stealing keys from my dad, trespassing on private property, and breaking into a pickup. All that was bad. I wanted my actions to seem good and right. I had to spin this in the right direction. We were just a couple of straightlaced boys looking for a way to be helpful and downright neighborly. *We were gonna fix this truck.*

I didn't want my sin to be sin; I wanted it to be righteousness.

We are name-changers. We grasp the potency of language. It's like we've all memorized *The Beginner's Guide to Giving Your Sin a Holy Name.* As I renamed my childish mischief "fixing the truck," so we christen our greed as "wise business sense" and dub our slander as "truth-telling." We talk of racism as "love of tradition." We identify adultery as "looking for our true soulmate." On and on it goes.

We also change the name of our ego-driven desire for recognition, our one-upmanship crusades, our selfish quest for satisfaction in what we accomplish all on our own. We rename it *ambition*.

Whitewashing a Dirty Word

Ambition has a sort of rags-to-riches story, only in this case it's a vice-to-virtue story. Look through the philosophical literature of the Greeks and Romans, read the Old and New Testaments, listen to the plays of Shakespeare, scan the pages of sermons and commentaries from virtually every leader and pastor in church history, and you'll find that ambition, far from being celebrated and encouraged, is warned against as a manifest evil.[4] Only in recent history has it undergone a metamorphosis from a dangerous vice to a celebrated virtue.

By ambition, I don't mean the get-up-and-go quality of a person who is driven to accomplish goals. Such an energetic approach to life is not only virtuous and healthy but it's built into us by the God who formed us to work with our hands and do good deeds. The Lord created Adam, after all, not to lounge around in a hammock all day in the shade of Eden's bower but to labor, to cultivate the soil (Gen. 2:5, 15). Working diligently, energetically, and joyfully to "get 'er done" (as we say in the South), is fully in tune with God's will for us. Proverbs urges us to emulate the ant, after all, not the sloth (6:6).

So the opposite of ambition is not laziness or apathy. The opposite of ambition is loving labor on behalf of the neighbor. Ambition, in other words, is self-seeking. It is not directed outwardly, in service to others, but inwardly, in slavery to ourselves. It's the passion to rise above others for the sake of our egos, to accomplish goals so as to polish our image, to view ourselves as more important than others, to crave the limelight, to be the star of the show. The ambitious person will work long hours, sacrifice much, and strive for excellence, all so that he or she will appear extraordinary in the eyes of others.

Ambition has morphed into a virtue. It's a quality applauded on TV, modeled in the movies, encouraged by commercials, exemplified by professional athletes. It's the attitude that drenches us in the cultural waters in which we swim. *Narcissism* is still a dirty word in modern society, but *ambition*, which is actually nothing more than narcissism at work, has been whitewashed.

We don't want our narcissistic labor to be sin; we want it to be righteousness. So we rename it ambition. A socially acceptable, even socially applaudable, quality.

Make It Your Ambition to Be Unambitious

Once again, now in the case of ambition and the quest for one-upmanship, we see how upside-down the Christian view of life is. For instance, Paul writes to the church in Thessalonica, "Make it your ambition to lead a quiet life: You should mind your own business and work with your hands, just as we told you" (1 Thess. 4:11 NIV). The Greek word for "make it your ambition" is from the verbal root *philotimeomai*, which means to aspire, to strive eagerly for, to glory or pride oneself in something.

Paul is being rhetorically sly, however, for he puts forward an oxymoron, a seeming contradiction. It would be like saying, "Gorge yourself enough to starve," or "Make so much money you'll be poor." Ambition and a quiet life, like oil and water, don't mix. And that's exactly Paul's ironic point: the follower of Jesus has such a different kind of ambition that it's no real ambition at all. It's an anti-ambition, an un-striving for personal glory. Make it your ambition, he's saying, to be unambitious.

He urges the same attitude when he writes to the Philippians, "Do nothing from selfish ambition or conceit, but in humility count others more significant than yourselves. Let each of you look not only to his own interests, but also to the interests of others" (2:3–4). The Greek word *eritheia*, translated here as "selfish ambition," occurs several other times in the New Testament. The word characterizes those who are "self-seeking" (Rom. 2:8) and engaged in "hostility" (2 Cor. 12:20) and "rivalries" (Gal. 5:20), and who, following the so-called wisdom that is "earthly, unspiritual, [and] demonic," harbor "jealousy and selfish ambition" in their hearts (James 3:14–15), leading to "disorder and every vile practice" (v. 16).

Needless to say, moms and dads don't want to foster *eritheia* within their children. Denominations don't want *eritheia* to characterize their congregations and pastors. Yet, when we encourage ambition, when we applaud the winners of a rivalry, when we inculcate within our children the attitude that they should rise above everyone else, that's precisely what we're doing. We are embracing and urging the practice of narcissistic behavior. We are conforming to the world, rejecting the countercultural wisdom of the Spirit, and—worst of all—missing out on what our Father wants to give us in Jesus.

The Unambitious Family

When Sunday mornings rolled around, rain or shine, regular or holiday weekends, we all knew where this family would be. All nine of them would be lined up—mom and dad, three sons, and four daughters—in the very back pew of the sanctuary of St. Paul's. I was the pastor of this small-town church, deep in the heart of Oklahoma. During my ministry there, I got to know my little flock very well. And it didn't take me long to realize that this family, the Maschmans, was actively involved in every aspect of our life together as believers. Only you'd never know it.

You'd never know it because they were a behind-the-scenes kind of family. Monday through Friday, Rich drove his old pickup to a nearby town where he earned a modest paycheck. And Jan not only took care of the children in their home but also cut and styled hair in the enclosed garage they'd converted into a beauty salon. In the life of the congregation, all those things that no one notices unless they're left undone, the Maschmans made sure were done. Mowing the grass, cleaning the church, cooking meals for families after funerals, doing the legwork to prepare for VBS, teaching Sunday school: you name it, they were in the thick of it.

They made it their ambition to lead a quiet life. They didn't seek a round of applause. They never asked for recognition. They were a salt-of-the-earth kind of family. Not extraordinary, not putting themselves ahead of others, not always posturing themselves to be the focus of attention. They embodied the ambition to be unambitious—to labor in love for others instead of working for themselves.

Ask any group of pastors and they'll tell you about the "Maschmans" in their congregation. Those families that have failed to be famous, failed to be extraordinary, failed to be ambitious—and because of those failures, have been successfully used by God in the day-to-day work of his kingdom. They visit the sick and pray with the homebound. Show up with shovels and rakes on congregational workdays. Scrub the parish toilets. Prepare the altar for Holy Communion and clean up afterward. Replace shingles on the sanctuary roof after a storm. Write notes to visitors. Teach second graders about David and Goliath.

You'll never see a feature story about them in the denomination's glossy magazine. No church history books will include a chapter about how many hours they volunteered, how many children they taught about Jesus, how many casseroles they baked for grieving families. They are the unknown, the unambitious, the unselfish saints without whom almost every aspect of a congregation's life together would come to a screeching halt. They probably don't even want me talking about them, but I beg their forgiveness. I'm dragging them out onto the stage for just a moment so we can remember who is behind the scenes. And so we can remember that, in God's kingdom, everything works backward. The unknown are known, the last are first, and little children are the models of exemplary greatness.

The Little Ones

Brennan Manning writes, "In the competitive game of one-upmanship, the disciples are driven by the need to be important and significant. They want to be somebody. According to John Shea, 'Every time this ambition surfaces, Jesus places a child in their midst or talks about a child.'"[5]

On the walk to Capernaum, for instance, the disciples were sparring back and forth about which of them was top dog. We can almost hear them arguing about who had the holiest Jewish pedigree, debating who taught Torah best, whose preaching kept listeners on the edge of their seats, who rubbed shoulders with Jesus at suppertime. Today, they'd also be humblebragging about who had more followers on Twitter and Facebook. As Bo Giertz writes, "It was a noble competition in Israel to see who was the most pious, who could withstand the most deprivation and whose faith was strongest."[6] Egos were at stake. Dreams were on the line.

But that evening, when Jesus asked them what they were discussing on the day's journey, they all acted like the cat got their tongue. Despite their earlier bravado, they knew how such posturing was antithetical to Jesus's mission. So they kept silent. And into this silence Jesus spoke.

"If anyone would be first, he must be last of all and servant of all." And he took a child and put him in the midst of them, and taking him in his arms, he said to them, "Whoever receives one such child in my name receives me, and whoever receives me, receives not me but him who sent me." (Mark 9:35–37)

My three-year-old grandson, Colt, has been staying with me and my wife the last few days. As I pour milk on his cereal for breakfast, open the heavy sliding back door so he can play in the yard, kiss away his tears after he face-plants in the dirt, and—yes—wipe his bottom after he's done on the toilet, I'm reminded of greatness in our Father's eyes. A greatness that consists of littleness, dependency, having nothing to boast about. In the face of Colt I see the face of Jesus, and in the face of Jesus I see the face of the Father, and in the face of the Father I see the God who hides himself in the low, the ordinary, the unambitious, the last, and the least. In my grandson I behold a living, breathing parable about the blessed failure to be somebody.

Jesus holds up children as models of greatness because they lack every quality of greatness the world lusts for. They can't boast prestige, power, influence, wealth, or wisdom. They command no armies and run no companies. They are easily overlooked and ignored, and all too often abused and neglected. No one tries to curry the favor of a child to get something in return. They have nothing of greatness to offer the world. Children are small, weak, dependent, always in need. As Bo Giertz notes, "A child was everyone's servant."[7]

Not despite these qualities but *because of them*, children are ideal models for the disciples of Jesus.

Children are what we pretend we're not. We waste so much of our lives pretending. We make believe we're independent when, without the involvement of thousands of others, we'd have no house to live in, no electricity for it, no clothes to wear, no car to drive, no road to drive the car on, and no job to drive the car to. We make believe we're strong and unstoppable when in reality a single bite from the wrong mosquito can put us in the hospital for a week. We pretend we're somebody when one bad decision can destroy our reputation, ruin our career, and wreck the façade of greatness we've labored so hard to build. Adults are all professional pretenders. The only thing great about us is the greatness of the lies we so greedily believe.

So Jesus puts a child in our midst. He shoves true greatness onto my lap in my three-year-old grandson. We see in children like Colt who we really are. And, more importantly, we see who we are in Jesus, the Father's Son.

I'll Meet You at the Bottom

We are free in Jesus to fail at being extraordinary. We are free in Jesus to fail at being ambitious, at making a name for ourselves, at ruling the world. We are free not to be supermen and superwomen, breaking barriers, earning trophies, and rising above our competitors. As the Father's children, as those who are secure in his love and acceptance of us in Jesus, we have nothing to prove to anyone. We have the approval of God himself. And, as Paul says, "If God is for us, who can be against us?" (Rom. 8:31).

True greatness is found in being the Father's son or daughter. True freedom is found in serving others, considering them more important than we are. And true success is found in the failure to find meaning and purpose in something we do, accomplish, build. Rather, our identity, our meaning and purpose, is not something we work for but receive from the hand of our Father.

What drives our ambition is, at its core, a hungering for love. If we do enough, if we accomplish great and extraordinary things, we will be loved. Like children in large families, we think we have to stand out to get our parents' attention. So we push past our coworkers, outperform our peers, leave everyone else in the dust—all to be noticed. That may make sense in the eyes of the world, and that may be the way to garner attention and even generate a following, but that's the exact opposite of what attracts God's attention.

Michael Horton writes, "While the first Adam launched a 'meet you at the top' philosophy of life, Jesus Christ says to the world, 'I'll meet you at the bottom.'"[8]

Jesus says, *I'll meet you at the bottom of anonymity, in a life hardly anyone notices and no one will remember once you're gone—no one, that is, but me, the only One who truly matters.*

I'll meet you at the bottom of a vanilla life, plain in its predictability, dull to most, but suffused with love for the unfortunate, sacrifice for those you love, and mercy toward the neighbor. I'll meet you in an ordinary nine-to-five job where every house you build, every engine you repair, every field you plow, every lesson you teach, is a good deed in which I rejoice.

I'll meet you at the bottom of a life of service, of considering others more important than yourself, of always asking what you can do for them instead of what they can do for you, of laying down your life for your friends. I'll meet you in this life patterned after mine, for "the Son of Man came not to be served but to serve, and to give his life as a ransom for many" (Matt. 20:28).

And, Christ says, I'll meet you at the bottom when you fall from the top, when the throne of ambition crumbles into dust and you shatter into pieces on the rock-hard ground of humility. I'll meet you there too, for "The LORD is near to the brokenhearted and saves the crushed in spirit" (Ps. 34:18). I'll meet you when your sycophants have deserted you for another idol, your fans have moved on to the next rising star, your reputation is trashed, your future is dark, and your great accomplishments are but dust in the wind. I'll meet you there and love you back to wholeness, to humility, to a life in which you'll one day thank me that you failed so miserably at being great.

Thomas Merton once wrote,

A few years ago a man who was compiling a book on Success wrote and asked me to contribute a statement on how I got to be a success. I replied indignantly that I was not able to consider myself a success in any terms that had a meaning to me. I swore I had spent my life strenuously avoiding success. If it happened that I had once written a best-seller this was a pure accident, due to inattention and naiveté, and I would take very good care never to do the same thing again. If I had a message to my contemporaries, I said it was surely this: be anything you like, be madmen, drunks, and bastards of any shape and form, but at all costs avoid one thing: success. I heard no more from him, and I am not aware that my reply was published with the other testimonials.[9]

Merton's words probably sound insane to most people, but he was keenly aware of the danger of success. He knew the risk of the full flowering of ambition. So he spent his life "strenuously avoiding success," focusing instead on a more excellent way: the way of humility and love.

The most astonishing, countercultural truth in the kingdom of Jesus is that love and acceptance have zero basis in worth or accomplishment. A billionaire in the Upper East Side in New York City is no more worthy of love and acceptance than the schizophrenic homeless man sleeping in an alley in the Bronx. Before any of us build a business or declare bankruptcy, before we earn a PhD or drop out of high school, before we establish a soup kitchen or star in a porn video, we are equally loved by the God who shows no favoritism. Our personal success does not attract his love, nor does our failure expand or contract it. The God who is love loves us indiscriminately, passionately, furiously. That love was on cosmic display when, atop a Roman tree of crucifixion, Jesus became the millionaire and the addict, the nun and the stripper, the newborn baby and the wrinkled octogenarian. All humanity—with its sores and wounds and twisted souls and barren lives and evil-infested pasts—he became, that all humanity might become, in him, resplendent in the eyes of the Father.

The cross proclaims that human success and accomplishment are meaningless categories to God. His categories are mercy and grace and love. Whether you are famous or unknown, filthy rich or living paycheck to paycheck, doesn't change the Father's acceptance of you, his sheer joy over having you as his child.

Way too much of our lives are spent chasing hollow promises that this accomplishment, this income, this trophy, will fill our lives with meaning and worth. The wisdom of God points us in a different direction: toward failure. The failure to bank our lives on achieving success. The failure to believe that we should dream as big as we want to. God grant that we fail at being extraordinary, being famous, making a name for ourselves.

Instead, may our Father make us like children. Aware of our dependence and littleness and frailty. Devoted not to getting ahead but to a life of serving everyone. Full of faith, hope, and love based not on what we have done, or some personal worth, but the riches of Christ's blood, shed in drops of mercy, to redeem us from a life of chasing after the wind.

Blessed are those who don't make a name for themselves but rejoice that their names are written in the Lamb's book of life.

3

Go Home, Heart, You're Drunk

The Failure to Follow Our Hearts

When my children were younger, we would sit to-gether on the couch before bedtime, Luke on my left and Auriana on my right, and read from our Bible storybook. Colorful illustrations graced one side of the page, and an abbreviated retelling of the narrative was on the other. One of their favorites was Adam naming the animals. The picture page showed elephants in tall grass, horses running through a field, and dogs playing. The story page described God's creation of Adam, the search for a companion for him, and how this first man chose a name for each of the animals that God paraded before him. My children delighted in the story. They basically memorized the narrative. But there was an ironic truth they didn't real-ize at the time.

As the biblical story goes on, the roles are unexpectedly reversed: the animals that Adam named become the animals that name Adam.

God often sends us to the zoo, the doghouse, and even the pigsty to learn about ourselves. David says his enemy is "like a lion eager to tear, as a young lion lurking in ambush" (Ps. 17:12). During Absalom's coup, David and his soldiers are described as "enraged, like a bear robbed of her cubs in the field" (2 Sam. 17:8). Israel is "like a stubborn heifer" (Hos. 4:16). As a "sow, after washing herself, returns to wallow in the mire," so we are prone to return to our pet sins (2 Pet. 2:22). God makes David's feet as stable as "the feet of a deer" on high places (2 Sam. 22:34). And over and over, God's people are depicted as sheep: prone to stray (Ps. 119:176), in constant danger from wolflike adversaries (Luke 10:3), and listening to the voice of their shepherd (John 10:27).

Tearing lions, angry momma bears, stubborn cows, muddy sows, sure-footed deer, straying sheep, and prowling wolves—in one way or another, these animals are icons of humanity. As Adam once named them, so now they "name" us. Zoology becomes anthropology.

I often think of this biblical background when I take my dog—or, rather, he takes me—for a walk. Justice is a nine-pound Dachshund, a miniature Weenie dog. What he lacks in size, however, he makes up for in the vigorous pursuit of adventure. Incapable of walking in a straight and narrow course—or unwilling to—he pulls the long leash to its limits and winds up corkscrewed around mailboxes, trees, and my legs. In the park he will race off the trail toward grazing bucks twenty times his size. He seems particularly to enjoy discovering random piles of feces and busting a move thereon in an impressive break-dancing routine popular among canines.

What I deem frustrating, dangerous, ill-advised, or just plain gross, to Justice is totally natural. He's just doing what dogs do. He is acting according to his canine nature. He is following his heart wherever it leads him—even if it leads to rolling in a pile of dung. And as such, Justice is a Bible dog. He is an image of humanity; specifically, a tiny, canine embodiment of the human heart.

The Hallmarkization of the Heart

We'll get back to that in a moment, but first we need to clarify what we mean by "heart." As we'll see, the heart David sang about in the psalms is not the same heart Pitbull raps about on our radios.

In the Scriptures, the heart is "the richest . . . term for the totality of man's inner or immaterial nature."[1] James K. A. Smith says to "think of the heart as the fulcrum of your most fundamental longings—a visceral, subconscious orientation to the world."[2] So, when you read about the "heart" in the Bible, don't picture the blood-pumping muscle in your chest cavity. Rather, think of it as the core of all you are—your thoughts, will, and emotions. Your heart is shorthand for what you feel, what you fear, what you love, what you desire, what you think. Very rarely in the Bible does it refer literally to the organ beating in your chest. It is, as Smith puts it, "the epicenter of the human person."[3]

That's the rich, biblical notion of the heart. And then there's its impoverished, stunted, modern counterpart. The meaning of heart has suffered an almost complete Hall-markization; it's been reshaped by media and marketing into little more than a dumpster of emotionalism. It's the go-to word in pop songs about hookups and breakups. Rather than the "epicenter of the human person," it's the cocktail glass swirling with a variety of moods and feelings. The popular notion of the heart is no longer the totality of our inner nature but just a single part of what makes us who we are: what we feel.

We need to keep this redefinition in mind when we talk about the heart. There is some overlap between the biblical and modern meanings of heart, but there's significant divergence as well. So with these differences in mind, let's talk about what it means to follow your heart.

The Rule of Joy-Sparking and KonMari

A few years ago, a Japanese cleaning consultant named Marie Kondo wrote *The Life-Changing Magic of Tidying Up: The Japanese Art of Decluttering and Organizing.*[4] The book not only skyrocketed to number one on the *New York Times* bestseller list but it even made the English dictionary one word longer. Thanks to this book, and a play on the author's name, we now have the verb *KonMari*.

The thrust of her argument is this: (1) we all have way too much stuff; (2) we need to minimalize and organize; and (3) here's how to do it. So far, so good. I don't know anyone who honestly believes another closet on the verge of avalanching with unused toys and unworn clothes somehow enriches our lives. We could all stand to haul a few loads to the nearest charity and organize what's left.

But it's Kondo's "how to do it" method that makes this approach unique. As you go through your belongings, you pick up each item and ask yourself a question: *Does this spark joy in me?* If it does, you put it in the keep-and-organize pile. If not, you thank the item for its service, then get rid of it. This is how you KonMari your life.

The question, "Does this spark joy in me?" is a fascinating way to judge the value of your belongings. In fact, some people have KonMaried far more than their shirts and shoes and high school memorabilia. In an article in the *New York Times*, "Marie Kondo and the Ruthless War on Stuff," the author records how one overly zealous woman decided to expand the decluttering of her life to her relationships as well. So she KonMaried her boyfriend. "Having tidied everything in her home and finding she still distinctly lacked happiness, she held her boyfriend in her hands, realized he no longer sparked joy and got rid of him."[5]

Who's next on the list for KonMarying? Spouses, siblings, friends, coworkers, pastors?

Now, of course, we don't go around saying, "I'm going to KonMari this," or "I'm going to KonMari that," since, well, that would be really weird. But the general tenor of her approach, often unconsciously, is an incredible influence behind many of the decisions we make. Like the woman who decided her boyfriend no longer sparked joy in her, we often apply this metric to relationships as well as responsibilities, vocations, and churches. We probably don't ask ourselves if they "spark joy" in us, but we do use parallel terms. We say things like, "I just don't feel happy in this situation anymore. . . . It's just not in my heart to continue this. . . . I feel my heart is leading me in another direction. . . . This just isn't meeting my emotional needs anymore," and so forth. In other words, wherever our hearts lead us, we go tramping after them like obedient slaves. We weigh pros and cons on a scale of pure emotion. We elect as our leader the least trustworthy, most self-serving, most terribly misguided guide imaginable: our own heart.

Therefore, to follow our heart, in our cultural parlance, is to do what feels good, what seems best for us, what meets our felt needs, what makes us happy, what completes us. In other words, what sparks joy.

In some rather benign cases, I suppose, that's fine. No harm, no foul. Perhaps we follow our hearts to a bowl of chocolate-topped strawberry ice cream or we follow our heart to embrace and kiss our spouse or we follow our heart into a job that dovetails with our skills and interests. In those situations, of course, there's nothing wrong with our decisions. We were hungry for dessert so we ate some (delicious choice, by the way!). We desired to express our love for our spouse so we did. We wanted a job that suited us so we found one. That's all well and good. Following our heart doesn't automatically equate to doing something wrong; it can mean we're simply engaging in activities that come naturally: fulfilling appetites, loving desires, and laudable goals.

The hazard with following our heart arises when this criterion becomes *the* deciding factor behind our decisions, when our heart trumps every other element in the decision-making process, and especially when "following our heart" leads to a narcissistic life where all that matters is our happiness, our satisfaction, our contentment, our fulfillment. To follow our heart, in other words, is often shorthand for running from God to chase after pseudo-gods, especially the idol of Me.

Just How Messed Up Are We?

In the background of this heart question is a much deeper question. We may have never asked it explicitly, but we've all answered it implicitly—and we daily, even hourly, pattern our lives after the particular answer we give. It's a serious and unsettling expedition that takes us to the heart (there's that word again!) of who we are. The question is anthropological in nature; that is, it's about human nature, what makes us tick. And our answer to it tends to determine our entire outlook not just about ourselves but also God and other people. It also determines how wise (or ludicrous) it is to let our hearts serve as our guides along the labyrinthine trails of life.

The question, to put it simply, is this: Just how messed up are we?

Let's sit down with a group of three friends—Randy, Charlotte, and Marty—and see what they have to say in answer to this question. I think they're fair representatives of the major viewpoints out there.

Randy: Well, here's how I look at it. We're all messed up in one way or another. Nobody's perfect, of course. We lose our innocence pretty early in life. And our family situations, peers, and life experiences shape us for the better or worse. Some people—like Hitler—end up as evil incarnate. Other people—like Mother Teresa—become living saints. Most of us are somewhere in the middle. Like Luke Bryan sings in that country song, "I believe most people are good." We're basically decent people who struggle with faults, fears, temptations, and sometimes addictions. But deep down we're okay. We're messed up, for sure, but not so messed up that we can't still choose right from wrong. I mean, we have free will, right? So we're in sort of a neutral zone, free to pursue good or evil.

Charlotte: I agree in general with Randy, but he's a little too negative for me. Look; yes, there have been awful people, freaks like Hitler and Mussolini and Jeffrey Dahmer. Nobody's denying that. But they're about .0001 percent of the human population. Most people are good, if not very good, by nature. Whatever faults we have are superficial. They're not really who we are. We may do some bad things but it's not like we're bad people. I believe inside each of us there's something like an ember of divinity, a glowing goodness that's just waiting to be fanned into flame. We have unlimited potential for good. We just have to believe in ourselves. Believe in our abilities. Believe that we can do it. After all, the only thing holding us back is ourselves. Our lives are in our hands to shape and mold as we see fit. So I would never say we are "messed up." We're all bursting at the seams with the potential for greatness and goodness.

Marty: While I respect both Randy's realism and Charlotte's optimism, I'm going to have to part ways with both of them and take us down a darker road. I think we're not just slightly messed up but royally messed up, shattered into smithereens, more broken than we can wrap our tiny brains around. On the surface we can learn to look good—even squeaky clean—and do good things, but deep down we're not good people. There's no ember of divinity glowing inside us. If there's any light coming from there, it's a bonfire of selfishness. We're a hodgepodge of anxieties, misguided loves, delusions of grandeur, self-worship, and—behind all this, driving most of our decisions—a phobia of dying. We're basically born as slaves to our passions and desires and stupid decisions. Even people who wind up being "living saints," as Randy said, are still messed up on the inside, still wrestling with their demons. Read Mother Teresa's diaries and letters. She fought these battles too. So, as much as it makes me feel great to think we're all basically good people, I have to echo the Good Book in saying the opposite: none of us are good, we've all sinned and fallen short of the glory of God, and we are born, by nature, as children of wrath. Say I'm a pessimist if you want. But I call a spade a spade. There's no sense pretending we're something we're not.

I'm sure each of these could be slightly tweaked to match other points of view, but I'd say these three positions are a fairly accurate portrayal of what the average person on the street thinks about how messed up we are. Personally, although I appreciate Charlotte's positivism, it sounds to me like she's lolled away too many afternoons on Pinterest reading inspirational memes, along with a handful of self-help books laced with questionable notions imported from Hinduism. I like Randy's thoughts best, not because they're accurate but because they still give me some wiggle room to work my way into sainthood by keeping my nose clean, making all the right decisions, and feeding the good inside me. Randy keeps things real but also keeps me in the driver's seat. Ultimately, he says, it's up to me to un-mess-up myself. And my control-freak ego finds that supremely gratifying.

And then there's wet-blanket Marty. Now there's a guy who knows how to rain on our parade. He's that "black fly in your Chardonnay," as the pop song says.[6] In our live-and-let-live world, Marty is unyielding, blunt, frank. He draws torturously clear lines. He's not bamboozled by the ego's whitewashing job.

And, like it or not, Marty's spot-on. At least if we're going to listen to God's thoughts on the matter. The Bible doesn't foster great expectations for humanity—unless by "great expectations" we mean the expectation of colossal harm. When the Scriptures answer the question, "Just how messed up are we?" they hem us in on every side. No escape. "God has shut up all in disobedience" (Rom. 11:32 NASB). Eugene Peterson's recasting of Psalm 14 perfectly sums it up: "God sticks his head out of heaven. He looks around. He's looking for someone not stupid—one man, even, God-expectant, just one God-ready woman. He comes up empty. A string of zeros" (vv. 2–3 MSG). A string of zeros, indeed. Everyone scores a big, fat F on God's Goodness Test.

It's this same song, second verse, with the human heart. When I'm reading the Scriptures, I like to take note of the initial occurrence of words, to see what kind of first impression they give as the narrative unfolds. So where does the Hebrew word for "heart" make its debut? It's six chapters into Genesis, when God is about to unveil his plans to flood the world and "wipe from the face of the earth the human race" (6:7 NIV). We read, "The LORD saw that the wickedness of man was great in the earth, and that every intention of the thoughts of his heart was only evil continually" (v. 5). The Hebrew word for "intention" is *yetzer*. It means inclination, imagination, form, or impulse. So it's not just that the thoughts of the heart are "only evil continually," but the very structure of those thoughts, their impulse, what shapes them, is also evil continually. And lest we assume, *Well, this only applies to pre-flood people since Noah's family reset morality to a higher level*, we read post-flood, after the ark is vacated, that "I will never again curse the ground because of man, for the intention of man's heart is evil from his youth" (8:21).

In other words, nothing really altered inside the human heart. The flood didn't re-virgin the unchaste heart. Indeed, in the very next chapter, Noah is discovered drunk and naked inside his tent, his youngest son gossips about it to his brothers, and when the patriarch wakes up he curses his grandson. The more things change, the more they stay the same.

This, then, is our first impression of the human heart. And it remains a lasting one. Much later in the biblical story, wise old Solomon will sum up the heart in this way: "The hearts of the children of man are full of evil, and madness is in their hearts while they live, and after that they go to the dead" (Eccles. 9:3). That might not be very uplifting, or meme-worthy, but it's the truth. And the truth is sometimes a bitter pill to swallow. Only by confronting it are we ready to move on.

Following the Heart of Jesus

But what are we ready to move on toward? To failure. To defeat. To becoming utterly incompetent at following our hearts everywhere they attempt to lead us. They are the blind leading the blind. If our messed-up nature is such that every intention of the thoughts of our hearts are only evil continually, then they are not only poor leaders but toxic ones.

What is the alternative? The one our Lord issues to his disciples of every generation, including our own: "If anyone would come after me, let him deny himself and take up his cross daily and follow me" (Luke 9:23). We can't afford to zoom past these words. We are prone to do that, of course, especially with verses like this one that many of us learned by heart in Sunday school. If we get in a rush, we're guaranteed to miss the upside-down nature of Jesus's words, the way in which they buck our bankrupt cultural system of thought, and how they carry us into a life of true joy and freedom in which our hearts rediscover their original love.

To deny ourselves is to say no to the entire universe we have concocted in our minds in which we rule over our castles in the air; become heroes of our own sagas, saviors in our own Gospels, and followers of our own hearts; and basically try to put Messiah Jesus on the unemployment line. To deny ourselves is to affirm that everything to which we say yes apart from God is sin. "Whatever does not proceed from faith is sin," Paul writes to the Romans (14:23). So the denial, the no, is total. A complete negation of the faux image of me as a pretty good person, a swell guy who messes up on occasion but isn't nearly as rotten as some people are.

Likewise, to take up our cross daily doesn't mean to shoulder our personal cares and concerns. Jesus isn't telling us merely to pick up our sicknesses, temptations, and other "crosses" of life and trudge along behind him. Immediately before he says this, our Lord predicts his upcoming passion. "The Son of Man must suffer many things and be rejected by the elders and chief priests and scribes, and be killed, and on the third day be raised" (Luke 9:22). Right on the heels of this, he says to take up our crosses daily and follow him (v. 23). In other words, Christ bids us follow him to death and the grave. That's what crosses are for, after all: to kill people. A hangman's noose isn't there just to chafe people's necks in uncomfortable ways; an electric chair doesn't simply jolt our bodies with stress. They kill. So too the cross, in Roman society, was an instrument with a singular purpose: executing people. To take up our crosses daily is to suffer many things with Jesus, be rejected with him, be killed with him, and on the third day be raised with him to newness of life.

To be a disciple of Jesus, to follow him instead of our hearts, necessitates our complete incorporation into him. He is not the typical first-century rabbi whom we copycat in our speech, study, and pattern of life. He is not an ethical or religious role model we shadow so as to become more like him. That kind of behavioral modification won't pass muster. Vastly more is needed. We must get inside him. Plunge into his identity. Be grafted into his body. Become so much a part of him that we become his co-crucified, co-resurrected brother or sister. So intimate with him that his Abba becomes our Abba, his head our head. And, yes, his heart our heart. We can't be followers of Jesus if we're outside Jesus. The only way we follow this rabbi is by ceasing to view ourselves as subjects and him as an object—we the "I" and he the "Thou." What we need is the I and Thou to fuse into Us.

And that's right down the Spirit's alley. That's what he does. He carries us outside Jerusalem, to Golgotha, though it resembles nothing like that blood-soaked hill. Calvary looks like a clear pool of water. And that it is, but also incredibly more. That pool of water, that place of baptism, is the doorway to Golgotha, our entrance into the execution chamber. "Do you not know that all of us who have been baptized into Christ Jesus were baptized into his death?" (Rom. 6:3).

We died in that pool of baptism, we died in Jesus, and our lives are hidden with Christ in God (Col. 3:3). "We were buried therefore with him by baptism into death" (Rom. 6:4). In that liquid grave we were also washed into Christ's tomb. But just as he didn't remain there, so we, in him, leave that chamber of death behind to step into the brilliance of Easter's hallelujah. Just as Christ was raised from the dead by the glory of the Father, we too "walk in newness of life" (v. 4).

To deny ourselves is to say no to a pre-crucifixion, pre-baptism existence in which we fake life while walking around, zombielike, "dead in our trespasses" (Eph. 2:5). To take up our cross daily is to live 24/7, 365 days a year, in a life that is no longer ours, for "I have been crucified with Christ. It is no longer I who live, but Christ who lives in me. And the life I now live in the flesh I live by faith in the Son of God, who loved me and gave himself for me" (Gal. 2:20). To follow Jesus is to become one body and one blood with him, bone of each other's bone and flesh of each other's flesh, in the marriage of the cross enacted in the nuptials of baptism.

Where Good Things Run Wild

The net result of the Spirit's work is astonishing. There's a world full of people blindly following their hearts down paths that can never bring true happiness and freedom into their lives. But in Christ a brand-spanking-new world unfolds for us—a world of freedom. G. K. Chesterton once wrote, "The more I considered Christianity, the more I found that while it had established a rule and order, the chief aim of that order was to give room for good things to run wild."[7]

In Jesus we are reborn into a life in which the good things run wild and free. The iron cages of fear and selfishness are demolished by the hammer of the cross. "If the Son sets you free, you will be free indeed" (John 8:36). He came to "proclaim liberty to the captives" (Luke 4:18). This is the "newness of life" that Paul wrote about (Rom. 6:4). Christ didn't hop down from heaven to be Moses #2, to shove us back under a life of ten more commandments or twenty more spiritual principles. He came to say, "In me you're free! I am the end of the law, the completion of the commandments. The fat lady has sung. It's over, done with, finished." There is therefore no condemnation hanging over our heads, no handcuffs on us, no ball and chain of religiosity we have to drag around to keep us in line. There's now room for the good things to run wild in our lives, because we're no longer enslaved to the notion that we have to toe the line to ingratiate ourselves to God. We're free to give our lives away, to lose ourselves in love, to actually forget about ourselves. Life in Christ is life in freedom, for we've already died and been raised again.

This liberation takes some getting used to. In fact, it takes a lifetime. The life of a follower of Jesus could be summed up in three words: *adjusting to freedom*. We're so accustomed to life behind bars that life beyond bars is frightening. Who'll tell us exactly what to do, where to go? No one. In Christ we are free from shoulds and oughts and musts. We are free to fail at slavishly following our hearts into places that might provide temporary pleasure but deliver lasting pain. We are free to fail at a life in which happiness is a god that promises much and delivers little. We are free to fail at running after what "sparks joy" in us, since those shallow, emotional joys never last long.

Follow the Lamb

I said at the beginning of this chapter that the animals Adam named became the animals that named Adam. But there is more: the animals whom God created also become those who provide a name for God himself. He is "the Lamb of God, who takes away the sin of the world" (John 1:29). In the nursery rhyme "Mary Had a Little Lamb," "Everywhere the child went, the lamb was sure to go." Not so with this Lamb. We follow him. Revelation describes the redeemed as those "who follow the Lamb wherever he goes" (14:4). It's really a rather outlandish idea when you picture it: a lamb leading people around. That's not the way things are supposed to work. But, as we have seen repeatedly, in the kingdom of God, the kingdom of this Lamb, everything we are accustomed to is turned upside down. We follow this Lamb. And he leads us through death into life.

The life the Lamb provides us is his own. We follow him, to be sure, but we follow him by becoming part of him. And in him we receive a new kind of heart—his own. A heart on which is inscribed the love of the Father. In Ezekiel, God promises, "And I will give you a new heart, and a new spirit I will put within you. And I will remove the heart of stone from your flesh and give you a heart of flesh" (36:26). The stony heart—heavy with guilt, always pulled downward to selfish desires, less-than-human in its addiction to triviality—is replaced by a true, human heart that beats in sync with Christ's. As well it should, since it's his own.

If the biblical notion of the heart is the "epicenter of the human person,"[8] then the epicenter of the Christian is the heart of Jesus. And if the heart of Jesus is there, so is the heart of the Father and the Holy Spirit. In Christ we become one with God, inextricably united with the Trinity. And in this union we discover what we've desired all along: true joy. Not the KonMari sparking variety of joy. This is the joy of being fully and unreservedly accepted by him in whom "we live and move and have our being" (Acts 17:28). The pure, unadulterated joy of living a life in which the good things run wild, where the shackles of fear drop off, and where we find rest in the God who delights in us as a Father and we as his children.

I've followed my heart into places that looked bright and inviting from the outside but within were dim and dark. There was always that "something" that was absent. Even if I felt okay, or even great, for a while, that feeling would fade. The emotional afterglow eventually darkened. And I was left, once more, lost, wandering around, destined to follow my heart into another dead-end street, another empty relationship, another titillating encounter, another hollow happiness.

In Christ I am, slowly but surely, adjusting to freedom. I'm learning that following him isn't about keeping spiritual rules or minding my religious p's and q's. Following him is about living in liberating love. Daily dying to myself and daily rising to newness of life in him. Daily dying to my old, stony heart and daily rising to find the heart of Jesus beating inside me. And I'm finding—as I hope you are—that though I can't trust my emotions, fickle as they are, I can trust the One whose heart is on full display atop the cross. I can trust that Lamb who takes away the sins of the world, including my own.

Our friend Marty is right. We are royally messed-up people. But as author Kimm Crandall titled her book, we are also a

Beloved Mess.[9] Loved by the Father who takes us in his arms, twisted and broken as we are, and creates in us clean hearts, breathes his Spirit into us, and pumps life into us with the blood of his Son.

Blessed are those who don't follow their hearts, for they follow the Lamb wherever he goes.

PART 2
OUR LIVES

4

Supermoms, Über Dads, and Other People Who Don't Exist

The Failure to Be a Perfect Parent

The town of Seagraves might qualify as one of the seven most unremarkable places in the world. It gathers dust in the far western portion of the state of Texas. Vast fields of cotton skirt the small community. They yawn toward the horizon, their rows as straight as the flight of a dove. The pump jacks of oil companies squat in these same fields. Their necks resemble iron pterodactyls, pecking the surface of the earth, up and down, up and down, sucking up the black gold.

If there are faces only a mother can love, then I suppose there are places only a local can love. And Seagraves is one of them.

Turn off Highway 83 as it passes through this 1.5-square-mile town, bounce along a couple of unpaved streets, and you'll pull up in front of a small, unpainted garage. Step inside and you'll see it's not a garage at all. It's an old, unoccupied single-room house. A kitchen/dining area hugs one side and a sitting/sleeping area takes up the other. Around back is a bathroom, an add-on when the family grew tired of shivering in the outhouse on January nights.

Put your ear on the faded, tattered wallpaper, close your eyes, and listen. Listen hard. Listen long. You'll hear a boy's voice talking excitedly to his mom and dad about a baseball game down the street. You'll hear a girl's voice going over what happened in school that day. You'll hear a mom shushing the children and shooing them outside as her husband sleeps after his graveyard shift. And you'll hear a dad's voice talk about how he and his coworkers scraped together enough cash to purchase an old car to share for their commute to the electrical plant. Absorbed into that wall are the tales of a family of four—loving, living, and scraping by in the 1940s and '50s. Absorbed into the wall are the tales of my family.

This tiny, one-room building is the house my dad grew up in. It's the house that built him.

Country music star and native Texan Miranda Lambert sings of "The House That Built Me."[1] She's lost her way in the world. Broken, confused, wanting to recapture who she once was. So she visits her childhood home—the home where another family now resides. She tells the new owner that those tiny handprints in the concrete of the front porch are hers. The back bedroom is where she practiced playing the guitar. Her favorite dog is buried beneath that oak tree. It is this house, with its deep and abiding memories of happier days, that constitutes the architecture of her soul. She's there to try and recapture those memories. Because this isn't just the house that her daddy built; it's the house that built her.

What house built you? What house is building your children? How is it shaping the architecture of their souls?

I think of that tiny house my dad called home in the '40s and '50s, the two houses I called home in the '70s and '80s, and the numerous homes that my children have grown up in. Three generations, three different narratives. My dad's parents married young and never divorced. My parents married young and recently celebrated fifty-two years together as husband and wife.

And then there's me. I too followed the family tradition of marrying young, only now, in my late forties, I have the skeletons of two divorces in my closet. My son and daughter have resided in four states at a total of nine different addresses. I and their stepfather are both on our third marriages. Their mom and stepmom are both on their second. If Miranda Lambert can sing of the "House That Built Me," my children can take a deep breath and sing of the "Parsonages, Seminary Houses, Apartments, Grandma's House, Rental Homes, and Regular Houses That Built Me."

Like most parents, I lug around an oversized suitcase stuffed with blame for the countless ways my parenting hasn't measured up. When I think of my children uprooted, rerooted, uprooted again, rerooted again, I blame myself. When I've watched them change schools, leave friends behind, and struggle to make new ones, I blame myself. When they've been angry, lonely, or depressed, I blame myself. You see the pattern, the ugly cycle. The houses that built them were not only numerous but fissured with divorces, break-ups, stepparents, every-other-weekend stays with Dad, and countless other issues that inevitably shaped the architecture of their own souls.

Every crack in the drywall, every leak in the roof, every chip in the paint, I trace back to my failed "if onlys" as a parent. If only I'd built and maintained a more ideal house—a divorce-free, fidelity-keeping, every-night-around-the-dinner-table, Mayberry kind of house—then my children would have been spared some of the emotional trauma they've endured. If only I'd been a more heroic parent, some semblance of a super dad, or at least an above-average father, then their lives would have turned out better. If only this, if only that. These are some of the silent, damning, finger-wagging sermons with which I harangue myself.

And I bet, if you're a parent, you've erected and mounted a pulpit in your own soul too. From it you sermonize yourself into guilt, shame, or regret about the string of if-onlys concerning your sons and daughters. They may be all grown up and lead relatively stable, successful lives, but nevertheless, you still remember "that move" or "that relationship" or "that huge, stupid mistake" that marred their childhood. If you're raising children now, you worry about making a mess of things, not doing enough for them, not providing enough, not raising them just right, not feeding them just the right foods, not getting them into just the right schools, failing them in a million ways. You look around at the house that's building your son, your daughter, and hope to God the tales absorbed into these walls are outstanding ones, that your children grow up and tell their friends or future spouses what an awesome parent you've been.

Despite all the mistakes I've made as a parent, I still find myself wishing the same. I want it to be easy and natural for my children to honor me. Don't you? Maybe, somehow, my children will see past my mistakes, forgive me, and tell my grandkids one day what a home-run dad I was. There's that part of me—that part of all of us—that won't let our dreams of parental heroism die. We won't be satisfied with being B− or C+ moms and dads. We certainly won't be humble enough to acknowledge we were total flops at the business.

We are propelled by the need, this ego-inflating desire, to be successful parents. Some of us, if we haven't been the best of parents, decide we'll make it up by being the coolest, most generous, sweetest grandmas and grandpas the world has ever witnessed. We're like Mr. Osborn in the novel *Vanity Fair*, who "tried by indulgence to the grandson to make up for harshness to [his son]."[2] Atonement for subpar parenting by superb grandparenting seems to be a relatively common self-salvation project. However we go about it, we're striving to build bigger houses that build better children. Be perfect parents or perfect grandparents. One way or another, our children will see us as a success. Who knows, maybe even God will come around to seeing us that way too.

I hope not. I pray God will make us all utter failures in these heroic parenting and grandparenting schemes of ours. Not failures in the ordinary sense of the term but the blessed kind of failures we've been discussing in these chapters. As we'll see, I suspect most of us have unconsciously adopted a skewed view of what a successful parent is. Worse, we've burdened ourselves with unrealistic expectations, set goals that no mortal can ever live up to, and—most disastrously— cut ourselves off from the only true hope we have as parents:

the mercy and love of our Father. His grace silences every "if only," burns our suitcases of shame at the foot of the cross, and is the only lasting bond uniting parent to child and child to parent. I hope we fail to be perfect parents, in other words, because it is only by acknowledging and embracing our failures that we see just how incredibly perfect is the rehabilitating love of our Father in heaven.

Straining toward Divinity

A couple of years ago, the Facebook page "Be a Fun Mum" posted this answer from Bunmi Laditan regarding "How to Be a Mom in 2017." She wrote,

> Make sure your children's academic, emotional, psychological, mental, spiritual, physical, nutritional, and social needs are met while being careful not to overstimulate, understimulate, improperly medicate, helicopter, or neglect them in a screen-free, processed foods-free, GMO-free, negative energy-free, plastic-free, body positive, socially conscious, egalitarian but also authoritative, nurturing but fostering of independence, gentle but not overly permissive, pesticide-free two-story, multilingual home preferably in a cul-de-sac with a backyard and 1.5 siblings spaced at least two years apart for proper development also don't forget the coconut oil.

Then she added this:

> How To Be A Mom In Literally Every Generation Before Ours: feed them sometimes.[3]

The post rapidly went viral. And with good reason. In those one hundred words, Bunmi Laditan, like the child in the fairy tale, had the audacity to point out that the emperor had no clothes on. She revealed the naked truth: how utterly laughable, controlling, prideful, heroic, impossible, and vain so much of modern parenting has become. If you want to qualify as a really good mom or dad today, simply being human won't make the grade. You've got to graduate to godhood. Be omnipresent in your child's life, omnipotent so as to give them every little thing they need, and omniscient enough to know precisely what to do in every conceivable parenting situation.

The downside of this attempted apotheosis is this: every time humans start straining toward divinity, we inevitably end up slumming in subhuman ways.

In season 2 of AMC's award-winning television series *Breaking Bad*, Walter White's son, Walter Jr., creates the website www.savewalterwhite.com to help raise money to cover the medical costs of his father's lung cancer treatments. When the Albuquerque television station hears about Walter Jr.'s efforts, and how donations have been flooding into the site, they sit down with the family to interview them. This is part of the conversation:

> Reporter: [Your father's] a good man, isn't he?
>
> Walter Jr.: Absolutely. Ask anyone, anybody. He's a great father, a great teacher. He knows like everything there is to know about chemistry. He's patient with you, he's always there for you. He's just decent. And he always does the right thing and that's how he teaches me to be.
>
> Reporter: Would you say he's your hero?
>
> Walter Jr.: Oh yeah, yes ma'am, totally. My dad is my hero.[4]

What Walter Jr. doesn't realize, of course, is that his heroic father is leading a double life. This high school chemistry teacher is making boatloads of cash on the side by cooking meth. In fact, the "donations" streaming into Walter Jr.'s website are from fake accounts set up by Walter's corrupt lawyer, Saul Goodman, to filter this illicit income back to the family. At this point in the show, his dad has already murdered two people, lied to scores of others, and is a rising drug lord in the local subculture, where he is known as "Heisenberg." He may be lots of things, but he is certainly not "just decent."

Walter, however, would look you straight in the eye and insist that everything he's doing, he's doing for the best of reasons: for his family. All the cash he's making will take care of them after the cancer takes his life. In his mind, Walter does envision himself wearing a cape. He's heroically doing what he thinks a man should do—indeed, must do—for his wife and family. He may be "breaking bad" in the eyes of the law, but he's breaking his back in doing good for those he loves. During another episode, while cradling his baby daughter, Walter pulls back some insulation to reveal two huge stockpiles of cash, hundreds of thousands of dollars, hidden away in the wall. "That's right," he coos to his daughter, "Daddy did that. Daddy did that for you."[5]

Only he didn't. That's just a smoke screen. He didn't do all that because he's such a loving, sacrificial, heroic daddy. Walter imagines himself to have graduated to godhood. He explains it to his partner with three words: "I am awake." When the cancer is discovered—rather the threat of death rousing him to the need for humility, faith, and love as a mortal man—it awakens him to a godlike potential, a prideful usurpation of his "destiny," and an uncompromising drive to beat death at its own game by leaving behind such an impressive material legacy that he will live on in the memory of his family. Instead of the imminence of the grave breaking his arrogant heart, it hardens it like adamant. Walter spirals downward into the paragon of bad parenting: a father who is so hell-bent on being a hero to his family that he destroys both himself and his family in the process. In straining toward divinity, Heisenberg ends up slumming in subhuman ways.

Some of my coworkers have nicknamed me "Heisenberg." I find this not a little ironic. I'll begrudgingly admit that with his glasses, facial structure, and facial hair, Walter could pass as my Hollywood doppelganger. But I can't say that I like the comparison. Not because of Heisenberg's looks but because of his soul. My coworkers, you see, are more right than they realize. They look to the outside but I look in my heart. And to be honest, there's an awful lot of Walter White lurking inside me. And, I suspect, you too.

We may never "break bad" in such an obvious, monumental way. We may remain upstanding, law-abiding citizens. Head of the PTA. Scoutmaster of a local Boy Scout pack. Sunday school teacher. But as parents, there's a diminutive Walter White running around inside our skulls, shouting, "Be awake! You need to be a tiger mom. You need to be an extraordinary dad. Your kids deserve the very best. Everything depends on your parental performance. Wake up and realize that one day you'll be dead, and you want your kids to look back on you as superhuman, an incredible parent who bent over backward to provide them with an ideal childhood."

In other words, our inner Heisenberg urges us toward infinitely more than "feeding our children sometimes." We must pretend we're demigods, superparents. We must point to our own "piles of cash," whatever that legacy might look like, and boast to our children, "That's right. Mommy and Daddy did that. Mommy and Daddy did that for you."

Plain Old Boring Moms and Dads

G. K. Chesterton wrote, "Of all horrible religions the most horrible is the worship of the god within."[6] He went on to explain, "Anyone who knows anybody knows how it would work. . . . That Jones shall worship the god within him turns out ultimately to mean that Jones shall worship Jones."[7] Lurking in the background of much modern parenting is this Walter White kind of worship. Adoration of the little god within. And the result? We act in less than human ways.

While we're going for broke in this vain, destructive effort, God's Spirit is at work within us to shepherd us in the exact opposite direction. That's pretty much what God spends all day doing. "We have met the enemy and he is us," as Pogo says. So the Spirit's ongoing work is rescuing us from ourselves, disassembling our plans, unmasking our inner gods as imposters, and pointing our feet down paths that look like failure but promise the true version of success—God's success.

God knows that if there's anything our world needs, it's certainly not more superparents. We need plain old boring moms and dads. The kind who are more concerned with modeling humble, loving service to their children than hothousing them into superbabies who out-SAT and out-GPA their classmates. The kind of parents who are more concerned with teaching their children "the joy of tasting tomatoes, apples and pears," as William Martin writes, than the thrill of guzzling the intoxicating liquor of success.[8] The kind of parents who are utter failures at perfectionism, at being heroes and heroines, at maintaining complete control of their child's upbringing—in short, who fail at being a god—in order that the grace of God might succeed in our lives as moms and dads as well as in the lives of our children.

Most of all, we need the kind of parents who see their primary identity not as parents but as children. Before I am a father, I am a son of God. Before my wife is a mother, she is a daughter of God. Before we are anything else—parent, spouse, worker, citizen—we are children of our heavenly Father. He has adopted us as his own in the waters of baptism. The family wealth is ours, for we are "heirs of God and co-heirs with Christ" (Rom. 8:17 NIV). The family name is ours, for the name of Christ and his Father is written on our foreheads to mark us as those who are redeemed (Rev. 14:1). In Christ, our daughters are also our sisters; our sons are also our brothers. We are all one family in him: one body, one blood, "one God and Father of all, who is over all and through all and in all" (Eph. 4:6).

This self-understanding as the Father's children becomes the foundation upon which we build our lives as parents. We don't wear capes; we wear the righteousness of Jesus. We aren't tiger moms; we are the Father's lambs. We aren't trainers of superkids; we are the beloved sons and daughters of the King. Knowing who you are in Jesus and knowing whose you are in the Father's family is not only the first step to Christian parenting but the second and third and fourth and final step as well. From the time we cradle our newborn babies in the hospital to the day we watch them walk across the high school stage—and even beyond that—we see ourselves as moms and dads second and as sons and daughters of God first.

My own mom must have understood this very well. She certainly modeled it that unforgettable day she found my *Playboy* magazine.

The Day My Mom Found My *Playboy*

When you're raised in a family where *The American Quarter Horse Journal* lines the shelves, where you're saddling horses and roping steers years before you can drive, then wearing cowboy boots comes with the territory. They fit well in the stirrups. They're good for walking through wet and muddy pens to get to your horse. And boots, as I discovered, are even tall and roomy enough for smuggling pornographic contraband into one's bedroom.

"I found your book," my mom said. We were sitting on the living room couch after school. I was in eighth grade. Puberty had not yet introduced itself into my life, but that certainly wasn't a hindrance to my mesmerizing fascination with the glossy images of unclad flesh that winked at me from the pages of *Playboy*. This was in the early 1980s, long before the internet and smartphones, where porn is but a click away. My friend's dad subscribed to the magazine, and, when no one was looking, I pilfered a back issue during a sleepover at his house. Stuck it in my boot. Snuck it into my house. Stared wide-eyed at the pages. And now I sank shamefully into the couch as my mom looked at me and revealed that while she was cleaning my room she had discovered my "book."

What's a parent to do? When you've caught your child in flagrant wrongdoing, when he's violated the rules of the house, when he's acting immorally, how do you address it? Do you say, "Oh, well, boys will be boys," and laugh it off as juvenile curiosity? Do you lay down the law, chastise him, and punish him with lawn-mowing, leaf-raking, and dish-washing for several weeks? What is the appropriate response?

I don't know that there is a one-size-fits-all answer to this. But I do know what my own mom did. And the fact that I can remember it still today, thirty-four years later, with gratitude and humility, says a lot.

The conversation was relatively brief. She wanted to know where I'd obtained the magazine and how long I'd had it. She informed me that she'd disposed of the material. And she also wanted to be clear that this would not happen again (it didn't). By this time my cheeks were flushed, tears were building up in my eyes, and a dark shame was soaking into my soul. It was bad enough that my mom knew I'd been looking at pornography. That she was actually looking me in the eye and talking about it with me was too much.

And then she said three words that I'll never forget: "You are forgiven." Not, "You are forgiven if . . ." Not, "You are forgiven, but . . ." Simply that unparalleled trinity of liberating words: "You are forgiven." Full stop. Seeing my evident anguish, having said more than enough to express her dis-approval, and realizing that my shame was already a self-inflicted punishment, she spoke not so much as a mother but as a fellow child of God. At that moment, she was my sister in Christ. A fellow beggar who tells another beggar where bread is to be found. The bread of absolution, the food of forgiveness, that I was hungry to consume. My mom, before she responded to my actions, first remembered that she herself was a child, a daughter of God, and let that merciful gift guide her own parenting.

What's more, she never brought it up again. She didn't hold it over my head. It was finished. My wrongdoing was forgotten, pressed into the open wounds of our fellow, crucified Savior, where it was absorbed by him who takes away the sin of the world, including the sins of lustful teenage boys.

I learned an invaluable lesson that day from my mom about how to be a blessed failure at parenting. My mom failed to treat me ungraciously. My mom failed to deal with me only as a hard-nosed judge. My mom failed to be a perfect parent who demanded perfect children. My mom failed to be a supermom. Instead, she was simply a Christian parent. She spoke to me as a fellow sinner in need of the same grace that she herself had received. "We are partners with our children," Elyse Fitzpatrick and Jessica Thompson write, "because we are just like them—dearly loved sinners."[9] As they write elsewhere, "At the deepest level of what we do as parents, we should hear the heartbeat of a loving, grace-giving Father who freely adopts rebels and transforms them into loving sons and daughters."[10]

I heard that paternal heartbeat echoing in the words of my mother that day when she said, "You are forgiven." It remains my earliest recollection of tasting the sweetness of grace. It also remains, in my mind, as a monument to my mom, who showed me, in just a few minutes, what some Christian parents never get around to realizing: that the greatest gift we can give our children is mercy. Morality is important. Education is important. Rules are important. Discipline is important. But there's absolutely nothing necessarily Christian about any of these. But grace and mercy in Jesus Christ? That's the heartbeat of Christianity. And that's what Christian parenting is ultimately all about: the failure to be supermoms and superdads and the success of living as fellow heirs, with our children, of the love of our Father.

The Seduction of Perfectionism

Perfectionism, in parenting and every other area of life, is a seductive ideology. It's what Brené Brown calls

> The belief that if we live perfect, look perfect, and act perfect, we can minimize or avoid the pain of blame, judgment, and shame. It's a shield. Perfectionism is a twenty-ton shield we lug around thinking that it will protect us when, in fact, it's the only thing that's preventing us from taking flight.[11]

Perfectionism in parenting is all about control. But control is just a mask. Beneath that mask is one of the oldest, ugliest faces around: fear. We fear that if we're not perfect parents, we'll mess our children up (don't worry, we will). We fear that if we don't control every aspect of our children's lives, they might get into trouble (they will anyway). We fear that if we don't hover over them, impress them, do heroic things for them, they'll not have the same advantages as other kids (so what?).

If there's anything we should fear, it's that we'll become so focused on perfectionism that we'll miss out on the joy of failure. We'll miss the opportunity to share the love of Jesus with our sons and daughters when they inevitably mess up. We'll miss the chance to shower mercy upon them when it's the last thing they expect or deserve. We'll miss confessing to them and asking for their forgiveness when we make bad decisions as a parent. If there's anything to fear, we should fear missing out on those opportunities, for that is when the love of our heavenly Father breaks into their lives. That is when we, along with our children, live as children of our heavenly Father. Let us fear endeavoring to be so successful as parents that we never need to admit we're sinful failures who need the same healing, divine love as our sons and daughters.

As of today, my son is seventeen years old and my daughter is twenty. Despite the fact that the houses that built them have been far from perfect, despite the fact that they've experienced firsthand the devastating effects of divorce and upheaval, both of them are healthy—spiritually, emotionally, physically. They're normal kids. They do normal things. They enjoy a normal life. Their parents have failed them in countless ways, but their Father never has. Indeed, he's even used our failures, our imperfections, our stupid and selfish decisions to shape our children into who they are.

I take immense comfort from this because it's a reminder of how insignificant I am. I am not the god of this family. I am not their hero. I'm no superdad. At best, I'm a mediocre father doing a mediocre job of "feeding them sometimes." The significant parent in this family, the one who does the real work of raising, teaching, watching over, and providing for them, is our Father in heaven. Every mother and every father is his mask, behind which he is at work. We are merely his servants, wearing not a cape or crown but the righteous robes of the Son by whose mercy we live and carry out the ordinary duties of our vocations.

To be a Christian parent is to be used by the Father to raise our children in Christ. Instead of pointing, in Walter White fashion, to all we've done for them, remind them of what Jesus has done for them. And, while we're at it, let's remind ourselves that Jesus did those same things for us. We moms and dads are also sons and daughters of the Father. The burdens of guilt we bear are the very burdens that Christ bids us lay at his feet. The accusations we hurl against ourselves for bad parenting are the very accusations he silences with three words: "You are forgiven."

The house that builds each of us—fathers, mothers, sons, daughters—is the house of grace, constructed from the wood of a Roman cross, decorated with the holiness of the Spirit, and inhabited by the Father who holds us all in his lap of mercy. The table overflows with the sweet desserts of the kingdom of God. The foundation will never crack. The roof never leaks. This is the house that Jesus built, the house that builds our lives, our loves, our identities. It is a house for failures who are beloved of the Father, in whom he rejoices as only an Abba can.

Blessed are those who fail at being supermoms and superdads, for they are forgiven children of our Father in heaven.

5

My Altar Has a Diesel Engine

The Failure to Search Out Our Calling

The year 1943 was a momentous year for two buildings. One is immediately recognizable. Every American citizen knows it, as do many around the world. The other? Only a sprinkling of people even remember it once existed. Very few could guide you to its weathered foundations. Yet it is the second of these structures that wove its way into the tapestry of my life.

In January 1943, in Arlington County, Virginia, directly across the Potomac River from Washington, DC, the headquarters of the United States Department of Defense was completed and dedicated. The Pentagon was born. A temple of power. A sanctuary of military muscle. An edifice inside of which innumerable decisions have been made that affected millions of lives and steered the course of modern history.

And it all began in the middle of World War II, in the opening month of 1943.

During that same year, thirteen hundred miles away, on the outskirts of a small Oklahoma town, a very different kind of building experienced a very different kind of event. If 1943 was the birth year of the Pentagon, it was the death year of a sanctuary. The *Deutsche Evangelische-Lutherische St. Pauls Gemeinde* (a mouthful, I know) was established in 1900 by a group of hardy, German-speaking farmers, along with their pastor, Joseph Timken. They saved and sacrificed to construct their first church building two decades later, in 1920. I'm looking at a faded black-and-white photograph of it right now. It was rustic but beautiful, a towering steeple at the front with rows of lancet windows gracing the sides. There it stood, this temple of grace, this sanctuary of the kingdom, for the next twenty-three years. Until 1943. Until a thunderstorm came rolling over the plains. Until an arrow of lightning shot into that towering steeple. Until all that remained was a pile of smoldering ashes.

Actually, that wasn't all that remained. While the church still stood, even as the flames danced above their heads, inside they ran. Farmers lifting pews. Women scooping up hymnals. Children grabbing what they could. Finally, four men hefted the altar from the front of the church, and, amid a fiery rain of embers and through clouds of smoke, they rushed it outside. As the bonfire raged into the night and board upon board dissolved into ash, the band of believers huddled in that red Oklahoma dirt around an altar that no longer had a church.

By the time I arrived, fresh from the seminary, to serve these believers, that fiery night was a faded memory in the minds of the oldest of the old-timers. The new church they had built in town had long housed the pews and hymnals and altar from their former sanctuary. The acrid smell of smoke had dissipated decades before. The altar bore a coat of fresh white paint. I stood before that selfsame altar, Sunday after Sunday, to offer prayers, to serve the Supper, to declare Christ's Word, to fulfill my vocation. But, for some reason, in the back of my mind, this altar always seemed to remind me of that night it had once stood under a roof of stars, in the dirt.

It had been an altar without a church.

Time like an ever-flowing stream has washed me downriver since those years when I stood before that altar. But it's as fresh in my mind as if I ministered before it yesterday. I eventually came to realize why I couldn't forget that it had once been in the dirt. Why it had stars for a roof. The Lord who governs my life with an unseen hand was impressing upon me even then that not every altar sits within a sanctuary.

About seven years after my ministry at St. Paul's, I craned my neck upward to gaze at the constellations. On this frigid February night, miles and miles from the artificial glow of town, the heavens were radiant with winking lights. Under my steel-toed boots was the soil of the Texas Panhandle, rich with petroleum and natural gas. A fifteen-foot hose snaked its way from a valve at the back of my semi to a fiberglass tank. I was siphoning off salty wastewater, a by-product of the gas well. A hard hat rested on my head. Leather gloves protected my hands. Above the pocket of my blue work shirt was the name of my employer, Turner Energy.

Suddenly, my mind returned to that fateful night when a lightning strike forced the altar of St. Paul's outside, onto the dirt, beneath these same stars. The memory just popped into my head. I now suspect it was the Spirit tapping me on the shoulder. Me, no longer a pastor but a truck driver. Me, no longer wearing vestments but hard hat and boots. Me, no longer holding golden Holy Communion vessels but muddy hoses and greasy wrenches.

The Spirit was reminding me that under the roof of these stars, outside a sanctuary, now sat another altar. A big one. A loud one. It had eighteen wheels, twelve gears, and pulled a forty-three-foot tanker. I served at it upward of seventy hours a week. This was a joyless epoch in my life, when I didn't do much smiling. But that night I did. I smiled toward the heavens and nodded my head in understanding. I was no longer in the official ministry, but I was still very much in the priesthood—the priesthood of the baptized, the priesthood shared by all believers in Christ. And my altar? My altar was a few feet away, a diesel engine rumbling under the hood.

More than a decade has slipped by since that night the Spirit tapped me on the shoulder to point to my new, noisy altar. During those years, that initial realization of my vocation as a priest of Christ, of the sacred nature of my so-called secular calling, has deepened and expanded. More importantly, it has turned my notion of labor upside down. I've come to see that so many of the assumptions we have about careers, employment, and vocations are in complete contradiction to the divine vision for our lives. In worst-case scenarios, they suck the soul right out of us, leaving us despising our jobs and living only for the weekends. It's high time for that to change. It's high time to recapture the sanctity of our callings and the priestly character of all our labor, as well as to realize that our altars have diesel engines, hold diaper bags, and support laptops.

What we need are failures on multiple levels: to fail at finding our calling, to fail at seeking fulfillment and purpose in work, and to fail at finding a secular career. What we'll be given, in those failures, is the success of the Spirit, the discovery of a life defined by loving sacrifice, and a realization of the rich variety of altars that punctuate our lives.

Do We Make a Living, or Does Our Living Make Us?

One of the unquestioned facts of modern life is that, sooner or later, every one of us must discover our calling. The sooner, the better. In my home state, for instance, middle school students are already being urged to reflect upon their interests and talents because, upon entering high school, they will be required to choose one of five paths of study. The academic pressure to choose a career field only intensifies as their senior year approaches. And, if they enter the university, it becomes imperative. They're hounded by stress-inducing questions. What do they want to do with the rest of their lives? What career do they want to pour tens of thousands of hours into? What do they want to be when they grow up?

If these are accepted facts of modern life, in premodern life they would have seemed rather pointless questions. By and large, pedigree determined profession. The sixteen-year-old son of a blacksmith in colonial America didn't face the existential crisis of deciding whether he would become a mechanical engineer or dot-com entrepreneur. He would, in all likelihood, be a blacksmith. Daughters followed in the footsteps of their mothers, sons in the footsteps of their fathers. What would your vocation be? Open your eyes and look around. See where you live, who you live with, and what they do. There's your answer.

And, in a way, that's still the answer today. That is, it's the answer if we revamp and realign our understanding of what *vocation* is. The English word is from the Latin *vocare*, which means "to call." A vocation simply means a calling. Unfortunately, however, we've left the word in the dryer way too long. We've shrunk vocation to mean only our nine-to-five job. How we make a living. And while vocation entails that, to equate career with vocation is like equating a tire with a car. It's only one small part of the whole.

This is critical to understand: our vocations are not how we make a living but how life has made us. Has life made you a son or daughter, mother or father, husband or wife, boss or employee, leader or citizen? Those are your callings, your vocations. And nobody has just one. On the day of my birth, for instance, I was a son, brother, and citizen of the United States. I wasn't even out of diapers and God had already called me into three vocations! Over time, I entered even more callings. I became a husband, father, grandfather, and employee. The premodern world had it right: open your eyes and look around to see where you live, who you live with, and what they do. There, written in the lives of those people, are your callings. God has summoned you to care for them. To love them. To sacrifice your time, your sweat, your dollars—all of yourself—to serve them.

To fail at finding our vocation is a blessing, because the quest to find it is in vain. It's not some deep mystery we have to solve by penciling in the ovals on career aptitude tests, searching our hearts, and attending job fairs. We can't unearth it because it's not buried. It's as plain as the face on our neighbor. We don't find our callings. Our callings find us. They are given by God in his creation of us, his providential guiding of our lives, and—most importantly—in the people he gathers around us.

We could spend hundreds of hours on our knees, praying that God would reveal to us exactly what career he would have us choose. The Lord has explicitly promised to give us wisdom when we ask (James 1:5). He's provided us with his Word to guide us as a "lamp to [our] feet and a light to [our] path" (Ps. 119:105). He's told us that whatever our hand finds to do, to do it with all our might (Eccles. 9:10). And he's promised to answer our prayers, lead us by his Spirit, and surround us with family and friends who can help us make prudent decisions. But he's made no specific promise to inform us, in no uncertain terms, which major to choose at our university, which trade skill to acquire, which career path would be best for us. He's left us free, as his children, to make that decision. God is just as happy if you choose to be a firefighter or an oral surgeon, a house painter or a politician. While our culture pounds away at the importance of which career we'll choose, such decisions elicit merely a shrug in God's kingdom. So you decided to be a rocket scientist? Sounds cool. So you chose to drive a trash truck? Great choice. Now, both of you, rocket scientist and trash-truck driver, remember *all* your callings. In the upside-down world of Christ's kingdom, the least important piece of paper we'll hold in our hand all year is our W-2. What we do with those hands the rest of the year in all our callings—in caring for our parents, our children, our siblings, our neighbors, our customers, our coworkers, our fellow citizens—is what counts.

God's Special Purpose for Our Lives

When I taught at seminary, I can't tell you how many casual conversations I had that went something like this:

Me: "So, how'd you end up here? What's your backstory?"

Them: "Well, for years I'd been working for such-and-such a company, making good money, advancing in the business. But I always felt like something was missing. There was this gap in my soul, you know, that my job just couldn't seem to fill. Like I'd somehow gone astray from the special purpose God had chosen for me. I wanted to do something more important with my life, something that helped more people. So, after years of procrastinating, I took the plunge. We sold our home, I quit my job, and here we are."

These conversations usually happened at the beginning of the academic year, over coffee, when incoming students met with professors. The plunge the students took was indeed a monumental one. Most were married, many with families, so their decision to uproot their lives and move across the country to study for the ministry affected more than just themselves. For the next two or three years the student's nose would be to the theological grindstone. If all went well, they'd graduate and be sent out to a congregation (or sometimes two or three congregations) to serve as their minister.

At some point during their ministry, most pastors fully realize a truth that they began to learn while at seminary: that God has no special, unique, individualized purpose for their life that they had somehow gone astray from before attending seminary. There was no gap in their soul that the ministry would plug. Being a pastor would not be something more important than being an accountant, police officer, or elementary school teacher. If they had stayed where they lived and not moved to the seminary, God would not have been disappointed with them. Yes, now they are pastors. So, yes, now God has called them into this vocation. But had they remained in their hometown, doing what they'd been doing, that would have been fine too. The Lord of the church would have used them there, in those callings, to serve their neighbor.

Going to seminary was a good choice. But not going would have been an equally good choice.

In other words, our seminary students achieved a failure: they failed to find fulfillment and purpose in what they thought would be the "ideal vocation" for them. The perfect job. The fairy-tale career. They learned a valuable lesson: that what we do for a living is not our life. How we make our money is not what makes us. What's listed on our résumé can never fulfill us, no matter how much money we make, how many people we help, how vitally important we think our work is. We need something else for that.

John Barnett, an Orthodox Christian, says that many years ago, the abbot of a monastery helped him understand this. He was at a point in his life when he was at a crossroads, anguishing over major decisions. Should he get married? Should he become a monk? What did God really and truly want him to do? He sought counsel from the abbot, who startled him with these words: "God doesn't care." The abbot then said, "God only cares that you seek first his kingdom."[1]

Our Father doesn't care, Barnett goes on to explain, "because all vocations, as the apostle Paul would have said, are 'lawful' (cf. 1 Cor. 10:23). God doesn't care because all vocations, in a sense, have been blessed."[2] What matters is not whether you seek to be a janitor or jeweler, spouse or single, priest or private investigator. Here's what matters: that you seek first God's kingdom and his righteousness (Matt. 6:33). Our Father will see to the rest. "Do not be anxious about your life, what you will eat or what you will drink, nor about your body, what you will put on," Jesus said (v. 25).

We could add, "Don't be anxious as to where you will work, which person you'll marry, whether you'll have children, if you have enough in your 401K, or the myriad other vain anxieties that so often suck the joy out of our lives." Oh, we of little faith. Our heavenly Father knows that we need all these things. But he also knows we need something more important: his kingdom. His righteousness. His grace and mercy. We need, in short, him. And if we have him, we have everything.

Included in that "everything" is freedom. We are free to marry or stay single. Free to have children or not have children. Free to pursue whatever career we'd like. As Paul told the believers in Corinth, "Only let each person lead the life that the Lord has assigned to him, and to which God has called him. This is my rule in all the churches" (1 Cor. 7:17). In context, Paul has been speaking about marriage and proceeds to talk about circumcision and uncircumcision, as well as servitude and freedom. His point is that the believers in Corinth—and us, today—must not suppose that becoming a Christian necessitates that we alter our external callings in life. "Each one should remain in the condition in which he was called" (v. 20). If you're single, getting married won't put you on the road to greater divine favor or usefulness. If you're delivering mail, quitting your job to become a missionary won't put you on the fast track to sainthood. Paul says that if you're a slave, and can obtain your freedom, by all means, go for it (v. 21). But even if you don't, know that in Jesus, you are a "freedman of the Lord" while the free person is a "bondservant of Christ" (v. 22).

What we are not free to do is to neglect seeking his kingdom. For in that kingdom is the only place where we'll find the fulfillment and purpose we're all searching for. We may marry the ideal spouse, but he or she won't be able to fill the void within us. We may land the dream job, but it won't quench our innermost thirst. Seeking fulfillment in our race or sex, culture or heritage, hobbies or passions, ministries or accomplishments won't do it. Inevitably, in one way or another, all these will fail us, because we were created for something else, something greater.

We were created for communion with God, citizenship in his kingdom, membership in his family. This fulfillment of our creation is received only in our re-creation in Christ, because in him we enter the good graces of our Father. We're like wandering children, lost and alone, knocking on a thousand doors in this world, looking for home. We think we find it here, only to be disappointed. We think we find it there, only to be let down. But when we knock on the door of Jesus, when he welcomes us inside his Father's house, then we step into our real home. There and only there is lasting joy and contentment.

We also discover, in our Father's house, the freedom to love those around us, whether they be family, friends, neighbors, strangers, or even our enemies. Not to love in order to get something in return. Not to love with calculation, loving only those who will love us back. In Jesus we learn to love indiscriminately, prodigally, willing even to "waste" our love on those who seem to deserve it least. And every place where that love is given, where we extend a helping hand, offer a prayer, do our job, that location of love is an altar where we serve as priests.

Altars as Locations of Love

The church, unfortunately, is not immune to the plague of buzzwords. Hang around a congregation long enough and you'll see the popular words and phrases rise and fall, only to be replaced by others as the religious jargon undergoes its incessant, infuriating metamorphosis. A recent post from the satirical site *The Babylon Bee* nails it with this article title: "Church Staff Learns Fresh Batch of Buzzwords That Will Be Meaningless in Six Months."[3]

I have an alternative proposal: instead of altering our language as predictably as Abercrombie & Fitch alters fashions, why not go retro and recover the language of the Bible itself? A fine place to start would be by speaking of believers as priests who offer their bodies as living sacrifices at the altars to which Christ has called them.

Peter says to the whole church: "But you are a chosen race, a royal priesthood, a holy nation, a people for his own possession, that you may proclaim the excellencies of him who called you out of darkness into his marvelous light" (1 Pet. 2:9). The apostle is borrowing and expanding ancient language from Exodus where God says that Israel is a "kingdom of priests and a holy nation" (19:6). We're accustomed to thinking of priests as a select group within the people of God. Priests, we assume, were the sons of Aaron in the Old Testament and are members of the ministry in some denominations today. The professional religious people. But just as we wrongly equate vocation with a job, so we wrongly equate priesthood with the pastoral ministry. Both are much broader and deeper categories.

Everywhere we look in the church, we see priests. Those noisy, energetic VBS students coloring a scene from Noah's ark—they are priests. The elderly gentleman who uses a walker to shuffle to his favorite pew—he's a priest. The youth group, the choir, the ushers, and the pastors are all included. Our ordination into the priesthood happened on the day we were baptized into our great high priest, Jesus. We became part of the "chosen race, a royal priesthood, a holy nation." We entered the sacred vocation that fundamentally changes the rest of our lives, that touches *every aspect* of who we are and what we do, every day of the year. It is this "every aspect" that deserves our attention.

We've grown accustomed to imagining our lives as a spacious room full of cubicles. Here's my cubicle where I work, here's my cubicle for socializing, my cubicle for family, for fitness, for religion. We shift between these numerous life-spaces quite fluidly, but as we do, we also operate with a more basic dichotomy in mind: sacred and secular. We have multiple secular cubicles (work, fitness, family, political, social) and only one sacred cubicle (church).

It's the same with time: with the exception of an hour or two of sacred time on Sunday morning, the rest of the week is secular time. Not only are believers quite comfortable with these partitions but nonbelievers are as well. We all have our spaces, our times, for secular activities—and, should we choose, sacred ones as well. It works quite nicely for everyone concerned.

It works quite nicely—that is, until we realize this slicing and dicing of our lives is all a big, fat lie.

For us, the priests of God, there is no dichotomy between sacred and secular. Monday morning's commute to work is just as sacred as Sunday morning's worship. Thursday evening's CrossFit workout is just as holy as Wednesday evening's small-group Bible study. Our prayers before meals with our family, our discussions with a planning committee at work, and our conversations over wine with friends are all sacred times for a priest.

"Secular" is a nonexistent category, because there is no arena of life that is off-limits to God's dominion, God's influence, God's kingdom. Nor are there neutral zones, where the Lord may or may not be active, depending on whether we opt to insert him into the situation by talking religion or doing religious stuff. Wherever we are, whatever we're doing, with whomever we're talking, we stand on sacred ground, doing sacred things, saying sacred words. The Spirit bulldozes our little manmade cubicles. He flattens our foolish, false dichotomies. When we become his priests, all of our lives are consumed and filled by the fire and light of the holy God.

This, then, brings us back to another aspect of vocational failure. As Christ's priests, we are utter failures at finding a secular calling in life. Whichever direction we turn, there's an altar awaiting us. On those altars we offer our bodies, our time, our energy, our possessions, and our words as a living sacrifice for those around us. This was the lesson that I began to learn in the Texas oilfields, as the Spirit opened my eyes to see that my new altar had a diesel engine.

I also began to realize that my trampoline, where I spent countless hours with my young children, was a bouncing altar. The stove where I cooked their meals and the table where I served them were also altars. I was no longer a pastor, but that didn't affect my priesthood one iota. God had called me to be a father, a worker, a son, a brother, and a neighbor, just as he's gone on to call me to be a husband again, as well as a grandfather. In each of these callings, I have particular, concrete altars at which I serve, as do you in the various vocations in which you offer yourself and all you have as a living sacrifice.

Wherever you are active in love for another, there is your altar of vocation.

In the congregation I attend, when a person is baptized they are given a candle to remind them that Christ is the light of the world. They are also given a white garment to help them recall that, in baptism, they are clothed with the pure righteousness of Christ. These little mementos are good. They are helpful. But perhaps we can give the newly baptized a little something different as well: a tiny replica of an altar. Just big enough to fit inside the palm of their hand. Let them take it home. Place it on a nightstand or a countertop where it can easily be seen on a daily basis. Let it serve as a visual reminder to those who have died and risen with Christ that they are now priests who serve at altars outside the church.

Where is your altar? Where do you serve as a priest? It's not a hard question to answer. Just pause for a moment to make a mental list of all the people who, in ways large and small, look to you for help, service, time, and love. There is your answer. There are your altars. There are the places and people where you engage in sacred work as part of the priesthood of the baptized.

Lori is married, a mom and stepmom, with two living parents and two sisters. She chose a career in dental hygiene, so she spends Monday through Friday with patients, dentists, and coworkers. She's also gone back to school to work on another degree, so she has professors and classmates. Lori's altars are the kitchen in which she cooks meals for her family, the bed she shares with her husband, the dental chair where she cleans teeth and educates patients, and the computer where she does her homework. These are the sacred sites of her priestly service. Holy ground. At each of these she is fulfilling a different calling or vocation. She is living out the life of the baptized by loving and caring for those whom the Spirit has called her to serve.

Adam is divorced, a father of one daughter. During the week he works in a tire distributor's warehouse. He also has two part-time jobs on the weekend: he mows a handful of neighborhood yards and is an Uber driver on Saturday nights. Despite his busy schedule, he also serves as assistant coach on his daughter's soccer team. Adam's altars are the table where he helps his daughter with math and English, the forklift he maneuvers to stock tires in overhead bins, the lawnmower he pushes, the car he uses to transport customers, and the grassy field where he teaches his daughter and other girls how to kick and pass the soccer ball. These are the places where he works as a priest. Sacred soil. In different ways with different people, he is serving as the mask of God, to care for those whom the Father has placed in his life.

Where are your altars? A bicycle, its training wheels removed, where you run alongside your five-year-old son as he gets his balance. An office where you make calls, answer emails, write software. An attic where you install a new A/C system to keep a family cool. A university classroom where you listen to lectures, take exams, and work toward your degree. A hiking path where you walk and talk with your friend who struggles with depression. A voting booth where you cast your ballot for the next mayor, senator, or president. Wherever

Christ is active within you to serve your neighbor, your family, your fellow citizens, your customers, your friends, or complete strangers—there is your altar, the concrete place where the Spirit is at work within you to bear his fruits, to sustain creation, and to fill you as you empty yourself into others.

In "The Freedom of a Christian," Martin Luther wrote, "A Christian is a perfectly free lord of all, subject to none. A Christian is a perfectly dutiful servant of all, subject to all."[4] This seeming contradiction perfectly summarizes our entire life as the priests of Christ. In Jesus we trample upon sin, death, the devil, and all evil. All of these lie vanquished at our feet, because our feet are in the feet of Jesus. In him we are "a kingdom, priests to his God and Father" (Rev. 1:6). "All things are yours" because you are in him "through whom are all things and through whom we exist" (1 Cor. 3:21; 8:6). In Christ we rule; we reign as fellow heirs of his glory and kingdom. All of this is ours by faith. We are perfectly free, lords of all, subject to none.

Not in spite of this *but because of this* we are also servants of all and subject to all. By faith we reign in Christ and by love we serve our neighbor. By faith we fill the heavenly throne with Jesus and by love we are emptied at the earthly altar of our neighbor's need. As Jesus says, "Whoever would be great among you must be your servant, and whoever would be first among you must be slave of all. For even the Son of Man came not to be served but to serve, and to give his life as a ransom for many" (Mark 10:43–45). That ransom, that sacrifice, was the final, fulfilling offering for sin. What we offer are "living sacrifices, holy and acceptable to God" because they are offered in Christ's holy and acceptable sacrifice of death (Rom. 12:1).

We count others more significant than ourselves (Phil. 2:3), serving all, subjecting ourselves to all, because in Christ we know that the first are last and the last are first. God doesn't need our good works, our vocations, our time or talents or treasures—our neighbors do. As Norman Nagel writes,

> We are priested not to offer sacrifices for our sins . . . but to offer ourselves. . . . We are living sacrifices whose lives are poured out in sacrifice to [Christ] where he has put himself to receive the sacrifice of our lives, that is our neighbor in his need.[5]

All our vocations pull us outside ourselves, direct us externally, to others who become the receptacles of our love and sacrifice and service.

In a world where the sacred is sequestered to certain times and places, Christ turns things upside down by permeating our lives with holy things, holy times, holy duties. In a world where it's left up to us to discover our callings, Christ creates us with vocations and brings us into still others. In a world where purpose is found in what we do, what we accomplish, Christ is himself our purpose, our goal, for in him we become fully human, fully alive. As priests of our God and Father, we fail to follow the wisdom of the world, we embrace the foolishness of our King, and we serve at altars that seem to lack all sanctity. Yet there God is at work, hiding in us as his mask, to continue to sustain his creation and pour his love into the world.

Blessed are those who fail to find their calling, for theirs is the kingdom where life and love and service find them.

6

Love Will Not Sustain Your Marriage

The Failure to Find Our Soulmate

The sun had yet to wink over the eastern skyline when the young man stepped out of the bushes, scanned left then right, and in six long strides was at the edge of the train tracks. The sliding metal door was slightly ajar. He threw his pack inside, took one more quick look around, and slipped in behind it. In the dark, he felt his way toward the back corner, slid to the cold floor, rolled a cigarette, and struck a match. He dug out his old blanket and wrapped it tightly around him. Might as well settle in and make himself as comfortable as possible. He was in for a long and lonely ride.

His whole life had been, in fact, a long and lonely ride. Raised on a farm on the outskirts of Waco, Texas, he'd learned early on the backbreaking labor of eking out a living from the stubborn, unpredictable soil. An injury on that same farm had paralyzed his right hand when he was still in his teens. During the drought years, when food was scarce and local jobs almost nonexistent, he'd hop on a train and hobo his way to the next town in search of work. This particular morning he was heading to San Angelo, where, if word from the grapevine could be trusted, he could earn some cash roughnecking in the oil patch nearby. Experience had schooled him in the art of begging cooks for food at the backs of local cafes early in the morning. Experience had also taught him that sometimes all you could do was tighten your belt another notch and wait for the next meal. The next train. The next job. The next long and lonely ride on this strange odyssey called Life.

I only met this wandering hobo once, when I was ten years old, but his adventures and misadventures formed part of the folklore of my family. He was my great-uncle, Ed Bird. Though he was born in the early 1900s, Ed was, in many ways, well ahead of his time. He was a man unrooted, on the move, always scouting the horizon for the next thing, whatever that might be. He drifted here and there, searching, seemingly on the hunt for something, actually for *someone*, worth settling down for.

There was a string of women in Ed's life—he was rumored to be quite the Romeo—but never a wife. He played the field, as we say today, during his bachelor years. Testing the waters, weighing the pros and cons of this or that lady friend in this or that town. What exactly was Ed looking for? What kind of ideal woman would embody the qualities requisite to be Mrs. Bird? Whatever they were, evidently no single woman possessed them. And by the time he had finished searching for this unique woman—what we might today call Ed's soulmate—it was too late. In his twilight years, Ed entered a nursing home. And there he would be till his dying day.

Yet, oddly enough, it was there, in Woodland Spring Nursing Home, in the small circle of residents, in the small town of Waco, finally rooted in one place, that Ed met the woman he'd been searching for. Her name was Mary Alff.

Ed and Mary spent countless hours together in the front lobby—two people with a lifetime behind them, recounting those long personal histories to one another, growing more inseparable by the day. After a few months, Ed finally did what he'd delayed doing for decades: he popped the question. And on November 3, 1979, residents of the nursing home and friends from the community gathered to witness as Ed and Mary were pronounced husband and wife.

I was nine years old when their wedding bells were ringing. Over the last forty years, as I've listened to and retold the tales about Ed's exploits, it's been eye-opening to gauge how his narrative has impacted me differently at different stages of my own life. When I was a boy, Ed rose as a mythical hero in my mind, a man with the whole world at his fingertips, unbound by convention, a noble hobo freelancing his way through life while other folks settled for yawning predictability. When I was in my twenties and thirties, Ed's bio seemed like a screenplay about a romantic man who was on a quest for the proverbial end of the rainbow, where the pot of gold would be a beautiful blonde with open arms and warm, inviting lips, who'd make all his dreams come true in the happily ever after of wedded bliss.

Then, in my forties, something changed. The stories about my great-uncle remained constant, but my perception of their message altered substantially. Ed, the godlike hero of my youth, shrunk into more of a tragic figure shackled by his own counterfeit freedom. Ed, the Casanova of my young adulthood, morphed into a regular Joe who twiddled his romantic thumbs so long they became crippled by arthritis. He became a man born too soon, because it seems Ed would have felt more at home in the culture of the twenty-first century than the twentieth. In many ways, his fear of settling down, his debilitating inability to keep his eyes off the horizon for that "something better," his chasing after that elusive "soulmate" he assumed must be out there awaiting his discovery, his perception of success and love in a relationship—all of these assumptions and hesitations made Ed very much a man of modernity.

Had Ed been born in 1995 instead of 1905, instead of squatting in the dark corner of a train car, he'd probably be relaxing in the airport, sipping a latte from Starbucks, waiting on his next flight. Instead of rolling a cigarette, he'd pull out his equally addictive iPhone, open the Tinder app, and see what romantic possibilities were just a click away. Two different scenarios from two epochs, but the original Ed and the modern Ed are simply different versions of the same man. Both are driven by identical desires, both travel the same emotional roads to meet those desires, and both have embarked on a fishing journey to find that one woman in the ocean of humanity in whose soul is the puzzle piece that will perfectly fill the gap in their own.

In a book about blessed failures, this chapter, above all, is the fruit of my painful failures. Because for most of my life, there's no way I could have written this chapter. What I assumed about love, marriage, relationships, and soulmates—all of it lacked depth and clarity. Not to mention biblical truth. And that led to a string of foolish decisions, failed relationships, and—as Solomon would say—"a chasing after the wind" (Eccles. 1:14 NIV). I may not have hoboed my way through life, as Ed did, but I hopped aboard countless relationships, only to end up in another one down the road. I too was chasing after that single, illusory individual who would complete me.

I never found her. I am now married to a wonderful woman named Stacy, but she's not my soulmate. Nor is she that one woman in the world who's the puzzle piece that fills the gap in my soul. She and I weren't meant for each other. Though she is a gift of God to me, she doesn't satisfy my every need and desire. I was certainly "in love" with her when we married, but I didn't love her. That would come later. And even when it did, that love has not been what has kept our marriage alive.

In other words, I have turned my back on Ed's trainyard, rejected his quest for Mrs. Perfection, and embraced divine, countercultural truths about love and relationships. I'm a complete failure at modern, romantic, love-sustaining relationships. And I hope you'll join me in being a blessed failure. Because in this failed state, we begin to realize that the wedded union of a man and woman—two people who are lifelong self-absorbed, self-protecting, self-centered sinners—will be unsustainable apart from Christ's grace, his work, his protection, and his forgiveness. To paraphrase the insight of Dietrich Bonhoeffer, it is not love that sustains our marriages; it is marriage that sustains our love.[1]

Cocaine and Falling in Love

In his book *Modern Romance*, Aziz Ansari discusses what he calls two "distinct types of love: passionate love and companionate love."[2] Passionate love is that warm and magical feeling we experience when we're "falling in love" with another person. What's fascinating, however, is not so much the wild beatings of the heart during this period but what's happening inside our heads. "During this phase your brain gets especially active and starts releasing all kinds of pleasurable, stimulating neurotransmitters. Your brain floods your neural synapses with dopamine, the same neurotransmitter that gets released when you do cocaine."[3] That's right: cocaine. It seems all those pop and country songs that compare falling in love with getting high are actually on to something.

And that's fine. Indeed, it's more than fine. Those initial mind-blowing, heart-palpitating "highs" we experience when we're drawn into another's life are a gift of God. They're part of our chemistry. That's how God made us. They're beautiful and pleasurable and downright amazing. But they also have a shelf life. "Scientists estimate that this phase [of passionate love] lasts about twelve to eighteen months."[4] At some point, the brain slows from a sprint back to a walk. We reenter normality. And then what?

Well, that depends. You could make the same blunder that Ed and I made. When that initial fire of passionate love begins to cool, you could misread that as a signal that love has faded, the relationship is disintegrating, and it's high time to move on and find someone new. Then the cycle will begin again. And soon end again. And on and on you will go, a relationship junkie, always chasing after that temporary euphoria of romance's budding phase. Ed did that for most of his life. I did it for far too many years. And countless men and women today are following this same exhausting, up-and-down, soul-shrinking path of addiction to "passionate love."

But there is another way, a better way. As Ansari writes, "In good relationships, as passionate love fades, a second kind of love arises to take its place: companionate love."[5] This type of love "is less intense but grows over time." It's associated, not with the pleasure centers of the brain but with those "regions having to do with long-term bonding and relationships."[6] This type of love has substance and longevity. It is not concerned with mountaintop experiences but with an extended journey through the labyrinth of life, with all its unexpected twists and turns, dark valleys, and boring marches through the colorless desert. Companionate love will relish its romantic sunsets, to be sure, but it will also face its dirty toilets to scrub, its snotty noses to wipe, its tears to dry. But it will do all these things not alone, nor with a string of relationships that fizzle annually, but alongside someone who has sworn to be our partner for life.

In other words, companionate love is what the Bible simply calls love.

In Paul's well-known and oft-quoted reflection on love, 1 Corinthians 13, there's a stark, implied flipside that one rarely hears mentioned. But without it, we miss the entire point of the chapter. The apostle writes, "Love is patient, love is kind. It does not envy, it does not boast, it is not proud. It does not dishonor others, it is not self-seeking, it is not easily angered, it keeps no record of wrongs," and so forth (1 Cor. 13:4–7 NIV). Lovely, poetic words, right?

Almost hymnlike in tone. But why is love patient? Because it often endures the beloved behaving stupidly and selfishly. Why is love kind? Because it suffers through unkindness and meanness from the one loved. Why does it not boast? Because love often weathers humiliation from the very one to whom its heart is devoted. Why does it keep no record of wrongs? Because if it did, there would be little time for anything but score-keeping and sin-tallying. This chapter on love is also the quintessential chapter on humanity's lovelessness. Paul is saying that when we love, we always love those who, sooner or later, will act unworthy of the devotion we give them.

That's why love is not something we fall into; it's a rough and rocky hill we commit ourselves to climb. Or, to change the metaphor, love is a story we decide to write together with another person.[7] There will be paragraphs penned in the calligraphy of pure ecstasy, but there will also be chapters scribbled in pain. The thing is, we don't know what form or direction the narrative will take. The final chapter is not written until it's lived. What we're devoting ourselves to is not a fairy tale, not a thriller, not a bestseller, but a simple story of sacrifice for someone else. We for them and (hopefully) they for us. But because it is the account of two sinners sharing the same bed, bank account, and bathroom counter, the narrative will become terribly messy and convoluted at times. There will be entire sections we wish we could blot out. Heated and vitriolic dialogues that embarrass us. And, along the way, plenty of happy surprises as well. We'll discover places in our hearts, and in the hearts of our beloved, that we didn't even know existed. That's the way stories unfold. Unpredictable. Boring. Beautiful. Ugly. Riveting. We'll find all of this and more when we commit to writing a story with another person to whom we say, "I love you."

I said earlier that I was *in love* with Stacy when we married, but I didn't *love* her. Our courtship was brief (okay, very brief): our first date was in January and we married in May. If the initial phase of passionate love lasts twelve to eighteen months, we were well into the second year of our marriage before we began coming down off that high. And we certainly did, like all couples do. Our brains stopped flooding our neural synapses with dopamine. The first chapter of our story together, written on cloud nine, floated back down to Texas dirt. The next chapter was about buying a house. And planning a budget. And enjoying a vacation to Colorado—in a tent, sleeping on the ground, alongside my two children. And more chapters were to come: joyful paragraphs about the births of Colt and Bowen, our grandsons; and heartbreaking paragraphs about the sudden death of Mike, the young husband of Stacy's best friend. There were times when trust was fragile. There were times when jealousy was strong. And there were times when the best thing we could do was simply to shut up, walk into another room, and say nothing at all until we both cooled off.

It was during these times, and only then, that I began to love her. And she began to love me. We chose companionate love, the real deal, love that demands we live outside ourselves, in the needs and hurts and ugliness of a very particular fellow sinner.

Love, to be love, must always be specific. It's quite meaningless to say we love people while we won't lift a finger to help our next-door neighbor. Or our spouse. In the concrete, normal, screwed-up lives we live, we learn to love. To love in speech and to love in silence. To love in word and to love in deed. And especially to love when the last thing we want to do is love, when the other person is being a jerk, when the romantic pool of dopamine in our brains is all dried up. Love doesn't really begin until the feeling of "falling in love" has faded, and we face the decision of whether we will become last so that the one we love can become first.

Yet, even as I learn what it means to love my spouse, I also daily and painfully learn how I fail at loving her. And she at loving me. If you're married—and you're even remotely honest with yourself—you face the same humbling realization. Your husband's little quirks that you thought were sort of cute while you were dating now drive you insane. So you hound him about them. When you were falling in love with your wife, you saw her blunt criticism of others as a sign of an honest personality, and you sort of found it endearing. But now it comes across as so petty and arrogant and condescending that you get in her face about it.

We harbored the illusion that we could change our spouses over time—improve them, alter them, mold them into the person we think they should be—and it didn't work. They're still the exact same flawed individual. So we get frustrated and angry and lash out. Or resort to passive-aggressive tactics. Or employ the silent treatment, the I'm-too-tired-for-sex treatment, or a long list of other relationship stratagems whereby we seek to force our will. In short, our love grows cold. Or lukewarm at best. Somewhere along the way, we'll likely ask ourselves if this whole thing was a terrible mistake and if we've wound up married to the wrong person. No one forewarned us the "for better, for worse" part of our vows would lean heavily toward the latter at times.

What have we discovered? Quite simply that our love cannot and will not sustain our marriage. Throw two sinners together, both congenitally curved in upon themselves, and force them by dint of circumstances to live for someone other than themselves, and you've got a powder keg in your hands. So there will be mini and major explosions, and plenty of pain when the smoke clears. Love will not be enough to keep us together. Even forgiveness will not be enough to keep us together.

There will come a time—likely many times—when, if our spouse were simply our boyfriend or girlfriend or live-in lover, we'd pack our bags, slam the front door, and march off in search of someone new and supposedly better. But we can't do that so easily when we're married. And if we have children, we're even more locked into the union. We find out that marriage is bigger than our egos, stronger than our weaknesses, and more stable than our shifting moods and seasons of unhappiness. Often we're also pleasantly surprised to find that, because we can't just hit the road at the first hint of marital problems, we end up staying and working our way through them. We hear each other out. Sacrifice our own desires. And learn to compromise, forgive, and learn that real love always entails bearing a cross.

We realize, in those words of Bonhoeffer, that it is not love that sustains our marriage but marriage that sustains our love. Marriage predates our fickle love and shallow commitment. Stacy and I didn't buy a marriage at Ikea and figure out how to assemble it after our wedding day. No couple does. God constructed that house long before any of us moved into it. We move into a reality established in Eden. As Robert F. Capon writes, "Entrance into marriage is precisely entrance into an already designed pattern of coinherence," that "built-in tendency by which all things seek to become one through membership in each other."[8]

We step into the vocations of husband and wife; we don't create them, shape them, or redefine them according to our whims and preferences. And thank God we don't. We'd make a terribly defective product. All efforts to redefine marriage—so popular and politically edgy today—are as vain as redefining the sun, the mountains, or water. They are what they are just as marriage is what it is: a fundamental, created reality that cannot be altered. When we marry, we step inside an ancient, divine structure that's bigger and older and more stable than our love or feelings or commitment.

It's also an ideal place, this divine house of marriage, to be a blessed school for sinners.

Hammering Square Sinners into the Round Hole of Marriage

The old marriage rites say that God has instituted marriage as a picture of the mystical union of Christ and his bride, the church. He ordained it for the procreation of children, as a remedy against sin (i.e., fornication), and for the couple's mutual society and help. All of this is biblical truth, of course. But there's more. As it turns out, marriage also happens to be a divine training ground for two people whose overwhelming desire is to live for themselves alone. Every man and woman, on their wedding day, is a square sinner whom God is just beginning to hammer into the round hole of marriage.

If we get our marital advice from Netflix, Nashville, the self-help section of the bookstore, or just about anywhere else in our society (including many churches), we'll spend our single years in hot pursuit of Mr. or Ms. Right. As Alain de Botton writes, we'll operate on the "founding Romantic idea upon which the Western understanding of marriage has been based the last 250 years: that a perfect being exists who can meet all our needs and satisfy our every yearning."[9] That person is meant for us and we for them. Our stories are written in the stars. This ideal individual is our one-and-only, the yin to our yang.

We'll discover this soulmate on the same day we spot the Loch Ness Monster while riding on a unicorn a few strides behind Sasquatch. They all belong to the same mythology. As Robert F. Capon reminds us, "The only candidates available for matrimony are, every last one of them, sinners. As sinners, they are in a fair way to wreck themselves and anyone else who gets within arm's length of them."[10] C. S. Lewis chimes in as well, noting that "Charity begins at home," but "so does uncharity."[11] In fact, at home, in private, with our spouse, is often the only place we feel like we can "be ourselves," which all too often, Lewis observes, means "trampling on all the restraints which civilized humanity has found indispensable for tolerable social intercourse."[12]

It doesn't matter if our marriage is an old-fashioned arranged kind or—like Ed's—the conclusion of a long lifetime of seeking, the result is still the same: when we say, "I do," we are bound, in a one-flesh union, to a deeply flawed person, and they to us.

> [They] will frustrate, anger, annoy, madden, and disappoint us—and we will (without any malice) do the same to them. There can be no end to our sense of emptiness and

incompleteness. . . . Choosing whom to commit ourselves to is merely a case of identifying which particular variety of suffering we would most like to sacrifice ourselves for.[13]

Now to those whose image of love and marriage is Disney-fied, all this probably comes across as maddeningly pessimistic, but I would urge that it's just plain ol' reality. Neither cheerful nor depressing—just the way things are in a fallen, fractured world populated by people who are also fallen and fractured.

A successful marriage, therefore, will be one in which God is hard at work on two egocentric sinners to help them fail at achieving their own wills that they might learn to serve the needs of another. As Gustaf Wingren writes,

The human being is self-willed, desiring that whatever happens shall be to his own advantage. When husband and wife, in marriage, serve one another and their children, this is not due to the heart's spontaneous and undisturbed expression of love, every day and hour. Rather, in marriage as an institution something compels the husband's selfish desires to yield and likewise inhibits the egocentricity of the wife's heart. At work in marriage is a power which compels self-giving to spouse and children.[14]

That power is God's power, channeled through the office of marriage itself. He's using this institution that he himself ordained as the means whereby he weeds out our selfishness and expands our love.

Marriage is a gift, but like many of God's gifts, it comes wrapped in a cross. It's the round hole our square-shaped hearts are hammered into. It manhandles us out of our little self-bubbles of ego-pleasing and into the sticky and needy life of a fellow sinner. We and our spouses are exposed to a life that doesn't revolve around us. There we die a little. We live a little. And we learn, by the teaching of the Spirit, that love and self-sacrifice are virtually synonymous.

The Ideal Partner

Today, as I write these words, it's Monday. Just like most days of the week, my alarm clock buzzes at 4:00 a.m. I hit snooze once or twice, stumble into the kitchen, pour myself a cup of very black coffee, and begin the process of awakening my slumbering brain so I can tap on the keyboard for a few hours. All of my writing is done in these dark, early mornings, secluded in my study, while most sane people are still sleeping. A little before six o'clock, I'll pour a second cup of coffee and take it into the bedroom to Stacy. I'll give her a kiss, whisper a "Good morning" and "I love you," and leave her to wake up while I go back to my writing before my time is up and I'm off to my day job.

She and I have a strong, healthy marriage. We talk and text throughout the day. We go on dates and vacations. We attend church. Every evening we enjoy a glass of wine and watch a little TV together. She is the best woman I know. She loves me, tolerates my flaws, doesn't hold my past against me, and is a wonderful mom and stepmom, a hard worker, an intelligent conversationalist, a faithful friend.

But as exemplary a wife as Stacy is, she does not complete me. And she knows this. She'll also tell you that I do not complete her. And if you are married, you and your spouse don't complete each other. To ask them to do so would be not only impossible but unloving, unrealistic, and a monumental burden they are not created to bear. As psychotherapist Esther Perel observes, countless people today say to their husband or wife, "Give me belonging, give me identity, give me continuity, but give me transcendence and mystery and awe all in one. Give me comfort, give me edge. Give me novelty, give me familiarity. Give me predictability, give me surprise."[15]

To expect all that from another person is not to ask them to be a spouse; it's demanding they be a god.

The only being who provides our lives with transcendent meaning, who infuses them with hope, who amazes us with mystery and awe, who loves and forgives us selflessly, who truly does complete us—that one Person is also a spouse. He is the bridegroom of the church, the husband of our souls, the embodiment of God. If there's a specific message that Christians offer the confused world regarding marriage, it is that the ideal spouse so many people are seeking is already married. But he invites us all to become part of his bride.

Paul writes that "Christ loved the church and gave himself up for her" (Eph. 5:25). He makes her holy, cleanses her by Word-drenched water, presents her to himself "in splendor, without spot or wrinkle or any such thing, that she might be holy and without blemish" (vv. 26–27). Holy and without blemish. Can you imagine that? Can you imagine a marriage in which one spouse makes the other spouse perfect, immaculate, complete? In Jesus, there's no imagining to it. It's no fantasy. That is precisely who we are in him, who we are because he has baptized us into being part of his beloved bride, the church.

What our society unrealistically urges us to seek in another person, we in the church already have in Jesus. Actually, we have profoundly more. He doesn't give us an emotional happiness that dissipates as the newlywed years wind down. He fills us with a joy that, even in the darkest days, remains intact because it is based not on our emotions but the activity of the Spirit. He doesn't make all our dreams come true but gradually empties us of all our selfish, destructive ambitions in order to replace them with desires that are in tune with how he created us.

If Valentine's Day is our society's ideal day to celebrate love and romance, then Good Friday and Easter are the church's days to celebrate what true love is and what true love does. For on those days, the husband of the church holds nothing back. He gives himself up wholly for us. His wedding ring is crafted from the nails that pierced his body on our behalf. The blood he shed becomes the righteous robe we wear. His victory over the grave is our victory over sin and death and everything that keeps us enslaved to this dying world. Crucified with him and resurrected in him, we are reborn as new creations who discover that everything we sought vainly from ourselves or others is found exclusively in him. Our souls are entwined with his own. We become one body and one blood with him. He completes us. And in that blessed completion, we become the people he desires us to be. Complete in him, we give ourselves in love to others. Perfect in his sacrifice, we sacrifice ourselves for the sake of our husbands and wives and children whom he has given to us in this life.

Blessed are those who fail at finding anyone in this world who completes them and who fail at sustaining their marriages by love alone but are completed and perfected in Christ, and whose marriages are sustained by the gift of Jesus and his limitless love.

PART 3
OUR CHURCHES

7

Building Walls and Digging Moats?

The Failure to Separate Ourselves

can leave my driveway and, in half an hour, roll into a sleepy town that boasts a Dollar Store, a post office, and a couple of gas stations. Around six hundred folks have sunk roots here. Like most rural Texas communities, tradition requires that you wave at fellow drivers. You dial a wrong number and end up chatting for five minutes with the other person. Everybody knows everybody. I grew up in a community like this one. There are thousands of them tucked away in the folds of the Texas landscape. Quiet. Slow-paced. Easily overlooked.

But on Sunday, November 5, 2017, the eyes of the world were locked on this one.

Around 11:30 that morning, Devin Patrick Kelley, armed with a Ruger AR-556, walked up to the First Baptist Church in Sutherland Springs, Texas. He began firing through the walls and windows. Then he stormed inside. For seven eternal minutes he stalked through the church, first spraying the worshipers with bullets, then slowing down to put the barrel to the heads of his victims, many of them children. By the time he left the sanctuary, ten women, seven men, and nine children (including one unborn) had been murdered. Another twenty were injured. One of the victims was the pastor's fourteen-year-old daughter. It was "the deadliest mass killing at a house of worship in modern U.S. history."[1]

In the aftermath of this massacre, the stories streaming from major media outlets were by and large predictable. They spoke of this tragedy as a chilling example of what can happen when mentally ill individuals are allowed to purchase firearms. Since a local resident shot and injured Devin Patrick Kelley when he emerged from the church, there were other articles about how "A good guy with a gun stopped a bad guy with a gun." Still others investigated the motives of the attacker, the bravery of the first responders, and the harrowing stories of the survivors. In a culture in which gun violence and mass shootings happen every few weeks—at churches, concerts, schools, and workplaces—such reports are depressingly commonplace.

But there is another story—a more foundational story—about the Sutherland Springs shooting that was not covered by a CNN or Fox News reporter. It wasn't told because it's not breaking news. In fact, it's news as old as the hills. This story is not about the shooter or gun violence or first responders. It's neither about human depravity nor heroic sacrifice. It's a story about First Baptist Church, to be sure, but more than simply this single congregation.

Open and Muted Hostility

The story that the Sutherland Springs attack brings to the fore is this: how the church of Jesus Christ lives in and interacts with a world that always, in subtle or subversive ways, is hostile toward it.

Sometimes that opposition is open and horrific. At the church in Texas, a deranged man vented his anger against the pastor and some estranged family members who worshiped there. Earlier that same year, ISIS suicide bombers entered two Coptic churches in Egypt and massacred over forty Christians gathered for Palm Sunday services. On June 17, 2015, white supremacist Dylann Roof murdered nine African American Christians at a church in Charleston, South Carolina. And we could easily, and sadly, multiply such examples from around the world.

Though the motives behind the attacks are sometimes personal, sometimes political, and sometimes racial, in the end the outcome is still the same: the kingdom of heaven suffers violence at the hands of those who stand in hostility against it.

It's understandable that horrific stories like these seize our attention. But they also deflect attention away from a different, more pervasive kind of hostility: a muted, subtle opposition to the church that seeks to subvert it. In fact, it frequently masquerades as friendship. A Judas Iscariot variety of friendship, where kisses betoken betrayal. In America, we witness an instance of this every four years, when political candidates court Christian leaders to seek their endorsement for the presidency. What they are really seeking is to transmogrify the church into a political instrument. (Just try to imagine Jesus campaigning for Pontius Pilate.) And to the extent that Christian leaders accommodate them, their hands are equally dirty. The candidate may win, but the church never does. It always loses. Loses its purpose, its integrity, its identity as a kingdom *not* of this world.

Here is muted hostility: an opposition to the church being a voice crying out in the wilderness like John the Baptist. Calling modern Herods to repent. Calling sinners into the baptismal Jordan. Calling the greatest and the least to come to "the Lamb of God, who takes away the sin of the world!" (John 1:29). To the extent that the church's arm is twisted— or its back scratched—to deflect its attention away from preaching the unworldly wisdom of the foolishness of the cross, to that same extent it suffers subversive hostility from the very world it seeks to save.

Between open and muted hostility are a thousand other varieties of opposition. All of us, every congregation and every believer, no matter what our cultural context, are barraged on a daily basis by -isms that are actually thinly veiled religions that seek to twist our hearts away from Christ and toward the gods of this world. Nationalism seeks our devotion to the generic god of country. Consumerism to the god of mammon. Egoism to the god of self. Hedonism to the god of pleasure.

Paul's sermon in the Areopagus of Athens could easily be modernized: "People of America, I perceive that in every way you are very religious. For as I walked through your malls, watched your TV shows, observed your politics, and examined your sports, I found altars everywhere to known and unknown gods" (Acts 17:22–23). All of these gods have their own kinds of liturgies, rituals, and sacraments by which they seek to win our hearts and to habituate us into an alternate way of life that is antithetical to the "faith that was once for all delivered to the saints" (Jude 3).

So how are we, members of the body of Christ, to live and work and serve in this world in which we are simultaneously citizens as well as "sojourners and exiles" (1 Pet. 2:11)? How are we to lead meaningful lives in our hometown and cities, while also "looking forward to the city that has foundations, whose designer and builder is God" (Heb. 11:10)? How is the bride of Christ to remain true to her Husband when she faces open or muted hostility? How are we to navigate our way through the maze of this world?

There's no shortage of routes that Christians have taken, from a marriage of convenience between the church and world, to an Amish-like separation from the prevailing culture, to a contemporary modification of the monastic mindset espoused in *The Benedict Option*.[2] The latter appears to be enjoying a growing popularity. Advocates of *The Benedict Option* would urge, for instance, that "it is time for all Christians to pull their children out of the public school system."[3] They also warn that Christians should think twice before entering the legal or medical fields because, in those vocations, they might have to choose between Christianity and their careers.[4] This option would even urge that, instead of swiping their Visa at stores owned by non-Christians, believers are "going to have to start building the Christian community's businesses through disciplined shopping—that is, by choosing to direct their patronage to Christian-owned enterprises."[5] In short, rather than fighting the flood of secularist opposition, shouldn't the church "build an ark in which to shelter until the water recedes and we can put our feet on dry land again?"[6]

Building arks in which to shelter, or constructing walls and digging moats around churches to protect them from the encroaching armies of ungodliness, may sound appealing at times. But it makes it rather difficult to "go therefore and make disciples of all nations" (Matt. 28:19). We can't be "always being prepared to make a defense to anyone who asks [us] for a reason for the hope that is in [us]" if we increasingly cut ourselves off from those who will inquire about that hope (1 Pet. 3:15). Since believers are the salt and light of the world, then keeping that salt locked up in an ark, or that light illumining only the inner rooms of an ecclesiastical castle, is a refusal to be who we are. It's a refusal to be who Christ has made us to be, to be the salt and light the world needs us to be.

Whatever opposition we face, open or muted, violent or subversive, the way forward is actually the way backward. Back not to St. Benedict and a neomonastic way of life inspired by his rule but much further. Back not to the sixth century AD but the sixth century BC. Not to Benedict but to Daniel; to Shadrach, Meshach, and Abednego; to Israel in Babylon. In the New Testament, Peter addresses his epistles to those who live in exile (1 Pet. 1:1, 17; 2:11). What better place to look, then, for wisdom on how to live as exiles now than to our Old Testament brothers and sisters as they lived in exile in Babylon? What we see is a surprising failure on their part—a failure to cut themselves off from the world, the public square, the marketplace of ideas. A failure, even, to steer clear of politics.

Rather than building walls in Babylon, they built bridges.

Building Bridges in Babylon

I made my first foray into Babylon as a young and inquisitive Baptist boy in a tiny Sunday school room in New Mexico. We visited this ancient place in the only "virtual reality" available in the 1970s: felt boards, coloring books, and skits. I once even played the part of Shadrach in a church play—a role that gave me the unwelcome nickname of "Chadrach" for years to come! Bloodthirsty kings, blazing furnaces, and dens teeming with roaring lions fired my young imagination.

If you were in Sunday school even a handful of times growing up, you too likely heard some part of Daniel retold. And if your classroom was anything like mine, the lesson taught was something along these lines: like Daniel and his friends, you too must bravely refuse to be polluted by the world. In other words, these stories were revamped into little more than biblical versions of Aesop's fables. Morality tales. Proverbial ethics. But they are far more than that.

To appreciate the context of Daniel, let's contemporize it. Imagine that four young American men, raised in church-going families, trained in biblical studies, scrupulous in their religious practices, are deported. They wind up halfway around the world, in a predominately Muslim country.

Over the next three years, they are cut off from everything and everyone they know. Even their names are changed: Matthew becomes Abdulla, Chris becomes Muhammad, Timothy becomes Yasir, and John becomes Shahid. They're taught the Arabic language, history, and culture. These four young men, who grew up reading the Gospels and singing "Amazing Grace," now study the Quran and hear the muezzin call the faithful to prayer. They also explore the political mazes and untangle the inner workings of the ruling families. These four young Christians are immersed in the Islamic world. Feel it. Taste it. Smell it. They are as far from their homeland—religiously, culturally, politically, linguistically, familially—as we can imagine.

Yet, despite this intense and ongoing attempt at their complete enculturation, these four young men somehow remain faithful, devoted disciples of Jesus. They still daily pray the Lord's Prayer. Gather in their little group to sing hymns every Sunday. Confess the Apostles' Creed. Follow the teachings of Christ. What's more, academically, they're at the top of their class. They outperform their fellow, non-Christian students. Over time, they are given governmental appointments, where their wisdom and insight prove invaluable to the state. One of them, in fact, becomes so prominent that the king makes him his chief advisor. Imagine that: a Christian becomes the right-hand man to a Muslim king!

If this scenario seems a bit farfetched to us, then so might the book of Daniel. What happened to our four fictitious Christian youths actually happened to four young Jewish men. They were deported from Israel. Given Babylonian names. Schooled for three years in "the literature and language of the Chaldeans" (Dan. 1:4). Entered "the king's personal service" (v. 5 NASB). And eventually were found, in wisdom and understanding, "ten times better than all the magicians and enchanters" in Babylon (v. 20). Daniel himself became a chief political advisor to Nebuchadnezzar.

They endured and achieved all this, however, while remaining faithful to Yahweh. They continued to observe the kosher laws (vv. 8–16). Even when three of them were threatened, and an attempt was made to execute them in the infamous "fiery furnace" of Nebuchadnezzar, they would not participate in state-sponsored idolatry (3:1–30). Later, when a decree was issued that forbade anyone to pray to a god other than the king, Daniel defied it, continued praying toward Jerusalem, and was cast into—and rescued from—the den of lions (6:1–28).

While it's remarkable that these four Israelites continued steadfast in their faith even in the face of martyrdom, that's not actually what impresses me the most. Most surprising is that they remained steadfast in the face of daily, even hourly, exposure to a culture pervaded by stories, music, rituals, habits, and assumptions that sought to un-Israelite them. To Babylonialize them. To habituate their hearts into a different vision of what life was all about, who God was, who they were as his children.

It's one thing to face the threat of death on a single day and remain strong. It's quite another to face unrelenting, ongoing attempts of a foreign culture to transform the heart yet remain believers in Yahweh and followers of his law, as well as successful servants in the political realm. By God's grace, Daniel, Shadrach, Meshach, and Abednego did just that. In their own time and place, they interacted with a world that was always, in subtle and subversive ways, hostile toward them.

Because of this, their stories, though two-and-a-half millennia old, are remarkably contemporary for us. Indeed, not only the stories of these four young men but the national story of Israel in exile is instructive. When Nebuchadnezzar conquered Jerusalem and deported the entire nation in

586 BC, they faced a new challenge: how to be the holy people of God outside the holy land. Believers living and working and becoming neighbors with unbelievers.

In a letter that Jeremiah wrote to the exiles, he gave them this basic counsel: *be fully present there.* "Build houses and live in them," he said (Jer. 29:5). In other words, make yourselves at home in Babylon. Sink roots there. Literally. Plant gardens in your backyard and enjoy the produce. Marry and have children and then grandchildren (v. 6). What's more, "Seek the welfare [*shalom*] of the city" where you live (v. 7). Devote yourself to the city's *shalom*—it's peace, wholeness, welfare, and goodness. "Pray to the LORD on its behalf, for in its welfare [*shalom*] you will find your welfare [*shalom*]." What's good for the city is good for you. You are enmeshed in the reality called Babylon. It's your new home—at least for the next seventy years and, for most of the Jewish exiles, for centuries to come.[7] So don't just make the best of it; make everything of it. Don't build walls and dig moats around a little Jewish castle in a pagan city. Build bridges. Be active. Be engaged. Be fully present in Babylon.

So the question for us is this: How can we be fully present in today's Babylon? How can we be the new Israel in our modern exile? We can practice the art of twin failure: failure to conform to this world and failure to cut ourselves off from it (Rom. 12:2).

Participation and Endurance

In the second century AD, an anonymous Christian wrote a letter to a certain Diognetus in which he described how he and his fellow believers fit in to this world.

For Christians are not distinguished from the rest of humanity by country, language, or custom. For nowhere do they live in cities of their own, nor do they speak some unusual dialect, nor do they practice an eccentric way of life. This teaching of theirs has not been discovered by the thought and reflection of ingenious people, nor do they promote any human doctrine, as some do. . . . [T]hey live in both Greek and barbarian cities, as each one's lot was cast, and follow the local customs in dress and food and other aspects of life.[8]

In other words, in a host of ways, Christians are mirror images of everyone else.

He goes on, however, to describe how, in other ways, Christians are not like everyone else, how they don't fit in to this world.

At the same time they demonstrate the remarkable and admittedly unusual character of their own citizenship. They live in their own countries, but only as nonresidents; they participate in everything as citizens, and endure everything as foreigners. Every foreign country is their fatherland, and every fatherland is foreign.[9]

The wisdom of this early Christian letter is encapsulated in this line: "they participate in everything as citizens, and endure everything as foreigners." This is "the remarkable and admittedly unusual character of their own citizenship." Participation and endurance. Fitting in while not fitting in. Resident nonresidents.

That second-century letter describes who we still are in the twenty-first century. And because that's who we are, we can fully expect to seem odd ducks to our unbelieving neighbors and coworkers. We can expect to endure ridicule at times. But not only that: because we participate in everything as citizens, because we "receive and eat with sinners" like our Lord did, we have countless opportunities to witness to them of the country that is truly and ultimately our home (Luke 15:2).

This witness that we give, this invitation to become co-citizens of the heavenly Jerusalem with us, is fostered within the culture of the church. Here is a key truth: the only way we are able to "participate in everything as citizens" is by ongoing participation in the life of God's people. I don't mean following a celebrity preacher on Twitter and Instagram. I don't mean listening to our favorite theologian's podcast or the local Christian radio station on our morning commute. I mean butts in the pews, eyes on the altar, ears attuned to the pulpit, mouths chewing the bread of the Supper, tongues red with Communion wine, hands clasping the hands of fellow believers, vocal cords singing hymns, knees bent in prayer. The only way we can be fully present in our modern Babylons is by simultaneously being fully present, bodily present, in a congregation we call home.

I didn't always buy into this line of thinking. For several years, in fact, I viewed the church like most of us view the dental office: a semiannual visit is more than enough. Plop down in the pew, let the preacher floss my soul, fix my sinful cavities, and send me on my way tsk-tsking about my need for good spiritual hygiene. I told myself that I was doing just fine without the church, without a pastor, without Sunday morning worship, without all that "organized religion" stuff. I did some Bible reading on occasion. Prayed before meals.

Knew that Jesus died and rose for me. But as for the church, I could take it or leave it. Most of the time, I left it.

And that left me virtually defenseless against an onslaught I didn't even realize was happening. I was trying to live in Babylon without a Jerusalem passport in my heart. I went to work, went shopping, watched movies, listened to music, dated and hung out with friends, and engaged on social media, during all of which I was exposed to what James K. A. Smith calls "a million microliturgies" that inculcated in my heart the belief that life was all about me, that promoted the religion of egoism.[10] I was trying to be a Daniel without praying toward Jerusalem three times a day (Dan. 6:10). I was trying to be like Shadrach without Meshach and Abednego, without the fellowship of my brothers in the faith, without a life in the community of believers. Most dangerously, I wasn't even aware of how thoroughly the religious undercurrents of our culture were deforming my heart and life. The longer I tried to be a lone Christian, without breathing the air of Jerusalem in worship, without soaking in her songs and drinking deeply of her streams, the more Babylonialized I became.

A huge part of the way our Lord rescued me from the shambles my life became was by planting me in a congregation again, under the care of a pastor, surrounded and encouraged by my fellow exiles. Not that this somehow automatically healed my wounds, patched up my life, and transformed me into a stellar disciple of Jesus. But it did for me what it does for all of us who participate together in the life of the church: it pulls us outside ourselves, plants us in the life of Christ, and connects us with the life of our brothers and sisters in the faith. We become smaller yet bigger—smaller in ourselves and bigger in Jesus. John the Baptist said of Jesus, "He must increase but I must decrease" (John 3:30). Yet the more we decrease beside Jesus, the more we increase in him. The more we die to ourselves, the more we live in him. And the more we live and increase in him, the more we realize that this is who we really are, who God has re-created us to be. Less is more: less us, more Jesus. But more Jesus simply means more of who we are truly meant to be.

Being more of who we truly are is also being failures: those who fail to cut ourselves off from the world but also fail to conform to it. This won't happen by simply thinking the right thoughts. Stuffing our brains with a list of orthodox answers to life's complicated questions is not a solution. We are more than the gray matter between our ears. More than "brains-on-a-stick."[11] The lies that surround us—and inhabit us!—are simply too sinister, too subtle, for us to assume we can think our way through the maze of life in exile. Babylon is after our minds, to be sure, but also our eyes, ears, stomachs, feet, hands, hearts—the whole of who we are as created beings.

Thus, the whole of who we are needs the whole life of Christ in his church. Our eyes to see the beauty of holiness. Our ears to hear sermons, Scriptures, sacred stories, and the songs of Zion. Our stomachs to receive the Lord's body and blood from his table. Our feet to stand within the holy place of his presence. Our hands to fold in prayer, raise in praise, and extend in greeting to fellow believers. And, through all this physicality, this tangible aspect of worship, for our hearts to be shaped into receptacles of Christ's grace and mercy, as well as conveyers of that grace and mercy to others.

Santa Claus, the Tooth Fairy, and the So-Called Secular

As we touched on in the previous chapter, most of us operate on the assumption that there are sacred and secular categories in our day-to-day lives. We engage in binary thinking: where two opposites are set against each other. One is this, the other is that, and ne'er the twain shall meet. So, for instance, we assume the church is sacred, but the state is secular (think of the oft-quoted "separation of church and state"). Or Sunday morning worship is sacred, but a Sunday afternoon trip to the mall is secular. Sermons are sacred, but movies are secular. Bibles are sacred, but novels and magazines and catalogues are secular. In our binary, this-is-not-that way of thinking, we have every aspect of our existence in well-defined, tightly sealed little cubicles.

On rare occasions in life we have eureka moments. Our eyes are opened to a new way of viewing reality. For me such an epiphany came when I realized that the categories of sacred and secular—or, perhaps better phrased, religious and nonreligious—were all a big, fat lie. A myth we have swallowed whole. Our common labels of "secular" or "nonreligious" are just as real as Santa and the Tooth Fairy. And, likewise, represent a childish view of reality that we would do well to leave behind.

David Zahl, of Mockingbird Ministries, recently commented during a conference lecture that "the problem in modern society is not that religion is on the wane but that we're more religious than we've ever been, and about too many things."[12] He pointed out the pervasiveness of current religiousness in our society, where our "golden calves" are named Parenting, Romance, Success, Personal Authenticity, and a myriad of other idols that demand our worship. His insight underscores the implicit religious nature of any culture. Wherever we go—to attend school, to shop, to watch sports, to hang out at the bar, to participate in a political rally—we are surrounded by speech and habits and songs that communicate their version of what really matters, who we are, what life is all about, what's important. In other words, hiding in plain sight in these seemingly nonreligious atmospheres is religion. Creeds disguised as "Just Do It." Parables masquerading as *Breaking Bad*. Ritual behavior called the Cowboys vs. the Giants.

Everywhere we go, we swim in a pool of religious assumptions. It's unavoidable. It's inevitable. It's challenging. But it's not the end of the world.

In fact, it is the true and ultimate end of the world that enables us to navigate our way through the religious fog of this world. To swim in this pool of religion without swallowing its chlorine-infused water. The end of the world is the return of Christ, the true and legitimate King. That final revelation of his current and ongoing reign over this world—and our hearts—is what gives us the perspective we need to live in the now-and-not-yet of this preresurrection life. Because the end of the world is secure in Christ, and we are secure in him, we can work and serve and play in this world as those who "participate in everything as citizens, and endure everything as foreigners."

That hope-filled end of the world spills backward into our life as the church here and now. We go "back to the future" every Lord's day. His reign and his kingdom, our resurrection and our everlasting life in him, become the guiding reality of our lives in exile. Every earthly power is deemed a lame-duck administration because their power is on the wane. They exist on borrowed time. "This world in its present form is passing away" (1 Cor. 7:31 NIV). Babylon's days are numbered.

But Jerusalem's days are not. "God is in the midst of her; she shall not be moved" (Ps. 46:5). The heavenly Jerusalem, which will come down from God on the last day, already comes down every Lord's day into our midst as we gather around his Word, his baptism, his meal (Rev. 21:2). In the Jerusalem of our local congregation we learn how to live in the Babylon of our local community. Our hearts are taught the love of God and neighbor, our eyes are directed to the face of our Father, our minds are set on things above, our feet are trained to walk in paths of righteousness, our hands are schooled in the sacrifice of service for those in need. In other words, we are immersed in true religion, the Spirit's piety. The more at home we are in the Jerusalem of the church, the safer we are in the Babylon of this world. And the more productive we will be in that Babylon, because we will live as those who know where our ultimate citizenship is.

We cannot avoid living in and interacting with a world that is always, in subtle or subversive ways, hostile toward the church. "If possible, so far as it depends on you, live peaceably with all," Paul said (Rom. 12:18). But know also that Babylon and Jerusalem are two kingdoms that will never merge. We live in both. And, by God's grace, we can be failures in this dual-citizenship: failing to conform to Babylon and failing to cut ourselves off from it. Like Daniel and his friends, we make it our endeavor to live faithfully in exile while awaiting that day when we will hear "a loud voice from the throne saying, 'Behold, the dwelling place of God is with man. He will dwell with them, and they will be his people, and God himself will be with them as their God'" (Rev. 21:3).

Blessed are those who fail to conform to this world yet also fail to cut themselves off from it, for they know their true citizenship is in Jerusalem above.

8

There's No Such Thing as a Personal Relationship with Jesus

The Failure to Have a Private Faith

One day, while working in his basement, a young man named Henry invented a product that would impact countless lives around the globe. He was twenty-one years old. The year was 1858. And the city was New York.

For much of its history, the Big Apple could have been nicknamed the Big Tinderbox. Fires, catastrophic ones, are burned into this city's collective memory. Five hundred structures were reduced to ashes in a 1776 blaze. Seven hundred more in the Great Fire of 1835. In Henry's time, about a million inhabitants were squeezed into this metropolis. Sharing space and sharing walls, as well as sharing conflagrations and their horrific aftermath. They needed someone to come up with a construction material that wasn't simply a fire waiting to happen. They needed Henry.

In his basement, using a clothes wringer, a tea kettle, and some tar, Henry Ward Johns invented the first fire-resistant roofing material.[1] That same year he would found the H. W. Johns Manufacturing Company. More products would soon follow.

The secret ingredient? A mineral. Not far from Henry's home, at the Ward's Hill Quarry on Staten Island, this mineral was being unearthed. And its seemingly magical properties were precisely what was needed to help fight the age-old problem of fires. When woven into fabrics, for instance, this mineral made them virtually fire-resistant. It was ideal not only for shingles, tar paper, and other roofing materials but also for theater curtains, blankets, aprons, pipe insulation, and much more.[2]

Our friend Henry had a good idea. A great idea, actually. An idea that faced a serious problem head-on, tackled it with a creative solution, and wound up revolutionizing lives.

Henry's idea also did something else: it killed him.

The mineral that was being mined on Staten Island, the mineral by which Henry impacted the lives of countless people in America and around the globe—that mineral was asbestos. And forty years after he'd come up with his product, that invention turned on its inventor.[3] In 1898, the coroner attributed Henry's death to "dust phthisis pneumonitis," commonly believed to be what we now call asbestosis.[4] Over time, a growing body of research revealed that prolonged inhalation of asbestos fibers could cause not only asbestosis but also lung cancer and mesothelioma. Thankfully, its use dramatically decreased. But by then it was too little, too late for far too many people, including Henry. Thousands upon thousands of human lives had been adversely affected by its use.

As with so many things, asbestos seemed like a good idea at the time.

The church also has a long and colorful history full of Henrys whose solutions "seemed like a good idea at the time." Many of their ideas also impacted countless lives around the world—impacted them, far too often, negatively.

The real sinister nature of asbestos, you see, is that it takes its sweet time to work harm in people's bodies. You don't breathe in the microscopic fibers on Monday, begin wheezing on Tuesday, and are six feet under by Friday. It may take twenty years for serious illnesses to surface. It may take fifty years. And all the while you'll probably assume things are just fine. Until they're not. Until hindsight becomes 20/20.

So it is with the church's Henrys. They may work or minister with the best of intentions, address real problems, and provide seemingly viable solutions. Their concepts, teachings, language choices, alterations, and programs may seem like good ideas at the time, but breathing them in eventually affects the hearts, minds, and souls of believers. And when huge swaths of Christianity are breathing this same air, the negative effects are simply staggering. Worse yet, these effects can become so widespread, so much the status quo, that they are rarely even noticed or questioned.

This chapter is focused on a single example of something in the church that "seemed like a good idea at the time"— but an example that's far from singular in its effect. We see its impact everywhere. It's relatively modern. It's cross-denominational. And it's theological asbestos. It's what we might call the Me-ization of Christianity.

The Me-ization of Christianity

In a famous, almost prophetic, article by Tom Wolfe in a 1976 issue of *New York* magazine, he described the 1970s as the "Me" Decade.[5] On the cover of the magazine were a number of men and women, all wearing yellow T-shirts, with "Me" emblazoned on the front. The picture itself is instructive: all are wearing the exact same shirt but all are also focused not on their unity, their togetherness, but on their individuality. *Me. Me. Me.* It's not a cohesive group but a collection of individuals.

Wolfe observed that the "old alchemical dream was changing base metals into gold. The new alchemical dream is: changing one's personality—remaking, remodeling, elevating, and polishing one's very self . . . and observing, studying, and doting on it (Me!)."[6] He saw the 1960s and '70s as the beginning of a Third Great Awakening. A religious movement like the two revival movements of the eighteenth and nineteenth centuries. Only this one was different:

> There is no ecumenical spirit within this Third Great Awakening. If anything, *there is a spirit of schism.* . . . Whatever the Third Great Awakening amounts to, for better or for worse, will have to do with this unprecedented post–World War II American development: the luxury, enjoyed by so many millions of middling folk, *of dwelling upon the self.*[7]

While this religion of "dwelling upon the self," personal improvement, and ego-elevating was happening in the culture, what was happening in the church? How were Christians responding to the problem of hyper-individualization? What kinds of solutions were the Henrys of the church offering to fight this fire that, more and more, burned away the cohesion of groups and generations? The church started talking more about the individual. More about the personal. More about Me.

In other words, the church fought this fire with gasoline.

We see a glaring example of this in the sudden appearance of a four-word phrase that, for many modern believers, defines the essence of Christianity. This phrase encapsulates where the church should supposedly focus her energies, her ministries, her sermons, her evangelism. As the Orthodox writer Stephen Freeman points out, "For many, it is considered the absolute minimum requirement for anyone claiming to be a Christian."[8] Without this, we're faking the faith. The phrase? "Personal relationship with Jesus." In Protestant churches, at least, one hears these words so often you'd think they were John 3:17.

Here's the surprising fact though: the phrase "personal relationship with Jesus" was virtually unheard of until modern times. In fact, if we search the Google Books Ngram Viewer for its occurrence in print prior to 1960, it's almost nonexistent.[9] But from the mid-1960s onward, it skyrockets.

And here's the vital point: this rapid rise of religious language that equates Christianity with having a personal relationship with the Savior *occurs simultaneously* with the rapid rise of cultural language in which everything personal begins to dominate that same landscape. The modern church begins talking about a personal relationship with Jesus while sliding into the Me Decade with its monomaniacal focus upon the self. This can hardly be a coincidence.

Just as Henry's use of asbestos was prompted by noble intentions, I'm sure the intentions of the church were good as well. They saw a problem and came up with a solution. After all, if society is all about the personal, all about Me, then the church can be all about the personal too—but in a Jesus sort of way. Instead of the religion of Me and my self-improvement, they offered the alternative of Me and my Jesus. "My own personal Jesus," as Depeche Mode would sing in the early 1990s.[10]

It seemed like a good idea at the time. And, for many, it still seems like a good idea. In fact, even to question the appropriateness of language such as "personal relationship with Jesus" often seems tantamount to heresy. Some of you are probably shaking your heads at me right now! But bear with me. We need to ask the hard, probing questions. Because this phrase, and the spiritual culture of which it is iconic, has reinforced the Me-ization of Christianity, a warped understanding of the church, a denial of basic human realities, and a Lone Ranger faith that looks nothing like what we find on the pages of the New Testament.

What we need, once more, is failure: a failure to foster a personal relationship with God. What we need instead, is to discover the relationship Jesus gives us within the body of his bride, the church.

Personal and Private

Let me, first of all, explain what I don't mean. I don't mean that Jesus doesn't interact with us as individuals. He most certainly does. Just as he called each of his disciples by name, so he calls each of us by name. He is the Good Shepherd who knows each sheep in his flock just as they know him (John 10:14). Just as the shepherd leaves the ninety-nine sheep to search for the one lost lamb, so Jesus will drop everything and come after each of us when we've wandered away. He wove each of us together in the womb, gave us each our own unique DNA. He died and rose again for every individual. Christ did this all for me. For you. For every single person. So, yes, Jesus relates to each of us as individuals.

I also don't mean that we should never pray alone, read the Bible alone, or worship alone. Yes, of course we should. Paul urges us to pray without ceasing, whether we're in a group or all alone (1 Thess. 5:17). When we're surrounded by fellow believers in a cathedral or kneeling alone in our bedroom, the God whom we address is "our Father" (Matt. 6:9)—or, to use the more intimate Aramaic word, our "Abba" (Gal. 4:6). My Abba, your Abba, our Abba. When we confess with our mouth Jesus is Lord and believe in our hearts that God raised him from the dead, we shall be saved, whether we do this surrounded by family, friends, and congregational members or surrounded only by mountains and pine trees on a solo camping trip (Rom. 10:9). When the Spirit shows us that we've sinned and fallen short of the glory of God, and when we cry out, "God be merciful to me, a sinner," our Father will hear and answer us with forgiveness on an individual basis (Luke 18:13; Rom. 3:23). Studying the Scriptures on one's own, as well as with others, is highly profitable. These sacred writings, which make us wise unto salvation, should be part of our daily bread (2 Tim. 3:15). Through them God feeds our souls individually as well as corporately, for by them we live "by every word that comes from the mouth of the LORD" (Deut. 8:3). And since we offer our bodies as "a living sacrifice, holy and acceptable to God," as our "spiritual worship," we do this whether we're alone or not (Rom. 12:1).

So, yes, without a doubt, Jesus saves Brittany, Thomas, Danielle, Charlie, and every other individual. He is my Savior and he is our Savior. My Lord and our Lord.

The problem is this: in the way we use language today, when we speak of a personal relationship, a personal Savior, a personal Lord, we almost always equate personal with *private*. Something that's focused on me and me alone. For my benefit and mine alone. For example, I hire a personal trainer to help whip my body into shape, not someone else's body. A personal banker helps me with my finances, not my neighbor's finances. My personal property is private property; it belongs exclusively to me and no one else. When a stranger stands too close to me and thus invades my privacy, I say they're in my personal space. Thus, rather than thinking of personal as the adjective implies—something relating to another person or persons—we are prone to twist it into an exclusionary word that revolves around the self.

Thus, a personal Savior with whom I have a personal relationship comes to mean this Savior and I have something no one else has. We've got a private thing going on that no one else is really involved in—or needs to be involved in. Our intimacy is unique and complete by itself.

As the old but ever-popular American hymn puts it, "I come to the garden alone[!] . . . And He walks with me and He talks with me and He tells me I am His own. And the joy we share as we tarry there, none other has ever known."[11] Alone; me, me, me. But, contrary to the hymn, others have indeed known and do know the joy of having intimacy with Christ, hearing him speak, walking through life with him by their side. These others comprise the church, the body of Jesus, of which we are all a part and by which we all belong not only to Jesus but to each other (more on that in a moment).

The Delusion of Independence

But there's another issue—a much bigger and broader issue—with the idea of a personal/private Savior with whom we have a personal/private relationship. We now operate on the assumption, not only in religion but in society and even in families, that the goal in life is for us to become independent, self-sustaining, self-protecting, self-providing individuals. So resourceful that we don't really need other people to help us. So comfortable in our own skin that we don't need the affirmation and encouragement of others. So strong that we don't need to lean on anyone else. So wise that we don't need someone else's counsel. So happy being Me that we don't need Us.

I am in control. I am my own man, my own woman. I've got my own back. I chart my own destiny. I am Mr. or Ms. Independent. I've got this, thank you very much.

Only we don't. And we're delusional if we think we do. No one, not a single person, is an independent, self-sustaining, self-protecting, self-providing individual. If there is a Great American Lie, this is it. God's goal for us is not to grow more independent but to grow increasingly aware of how dependent we are on him and on others for everything. Rather than our living private lives concerned with personal things, God calls us outside ourselves, into a cosmic web of interconnected relationships that span heaven and earth.

To realize this, all we need to do is wake up in the morning and begin, at that very moment, to ask ourselves, step by step through the day, if we could do anything without someone else having a hand in it. We open our eyes in a bed that someone else built, inside a room and a house that others constructed. We pour a cup of coffee made from beans that a thousand hands were involved in growing, harvesting, transporting, and selling. We drive to work in a vehicle that is the product of over a century of research, experimentation, and engineering that required millions upon millions of people's minds and bodies to make.

Did we pave the highway we drive on or drill for the fossil fuels that power the car? Did we design and erect the building in which we work? The computer and phone we use? Did we grow the lettuce and tomatoes on our hamburger or raise the cow that provided the beef? We can't even use the restroom without countless people's involvement in making toilets, producing toilet paper, managing sewer systems, and making plumbing repairs. In fact, for about 60 percent of the population, even reading these words would be impossible without the doctors and specialists who provided you with the right glasses or contacts to correct your vision. Unless we're prepared to move deep into the wilderness, sew clothing from animal hides, grow all our own food, make all our own medicines from roots and herbs, fashion all our own tools and weapons, and live alone until the day we die, we are a far cry from independent.

Therefore, we can talk all day long about me, me, me, but every moment of every day, even in the miniscule details of our lives, we exist in a world in which it's impossible to survive, much less thrive, without us, us, us.

This should come as no surprise to those familiar with the biblical story. The very first time that God said something was "not good" was when someone was alone. The earth was good. The heavens were good. The animals and seas and mountains were good. But Adam, all on his lonesome,

without another human being, without someone to comple-
ment him, live with him, and be his family, his helper, his
own flesh and blood—that was not good at all. A private
Adam who had a personal relationship with his Creator was
simply not going to cut it. He may have been a glorious,
regal, beautiful human being, but he was still not independent. Therefore God gave him Eve, built from his own body.
He belonged to her and she to him. They depended on each
other, leaned on each other, found fulfillment in each other.

Humanity was not truly complete until singular had expanded into plural, until I had become We.

Beauty in Community

The We of Adam and Eve would, over time, become the
human family, a cosmic community, full of variation but
united in nature. From the Genesis perspective, every man I
meet is my brother, every woman my sister, whatever racial
or national distinctions we might have. We all are created in
the image of God. We all are those for whom Christ died. We
all trace our family trees back to one seed, planted in Eden
long ago. In every person's face I see a mirror of my own.
Their humanity is exactly like mine. As Isaiah says, when we
observe any person in need, we see our "own flesh" (58:7).

But within this human family is a smaller family, a group
that is bound into an even more tightly knit community. It's
been around since the beginning. In the biblical narrative, it
goes by different names: Israel, Jacob, the household of God,
the saints, the chosen, the way, the church of God, the church
of Christ, the flock of God, the bride of Christ, the body of
Christ. Whatever name we might choose, the reality is still

the same: it's the family of God in which we all share the same Spirit, call upon the same Father, and stand alongside the same brother, Jesus.

Since the church is a family, this means that our life together will sometimes be beautiful and sometimes ugly. That's how families are, right? The best and the worst. We don't always get along. We bicker and sulk and say nasty things at family get-togethers. But we also laugh and dance and forgive and share meals together. We listen to Grandpa's war stories. We help our cousin when he's down on his luck. We try to reconcile Aunt Susan and her son Ryan when they're quarreling about something. We may not always get along with everyone in our family, but they remain our family. We don't get to choose them. We're born into them. Without the bare bones of a family—a mom and a dad—none of us would even exist. It took two people to make one of me. So from the very moment of my conception, I was already connected to two other people. I was in a family while still in the womb. I was always a We.

So it is in the family called the church. Paul tells the Galatians that the "Jerusalem above is . . . our mother" (Gal. 4:26). In the third century, Cyprian of Carthage famously wrote, "He can no longer have God for his Father, who has not the church for his mother."[12] He added, "From her womb we are born, by her milk we are nourished, by her spirit we are animated." In this sense, a Christian orphan is a contradiction in terms. Believers cannot be orphans because their mother—the church—and their Father—God himself—cannot die. We all enter the family of God from the womb of the church. As Cyprian says, the milk of the Word she preaches and teaches nourishes us. Her spirit of grace and forgiveness and wisdom enlivens us. She may be nicknamed Baptist or Catholic, Orthodox or Pentecostal, but her true name is what the Nicene Creed calls the "one holy catholic and apostolic church."

All our brothers and sisters, our whole Christian family, are born from this same womb. We are a big, diverse, cosmopolitan family. But there is one thing we are not: we are not on our own. We don't have a personal relationship with God—at least, not in the way that is ordinarily understood. There is no just-me-and-Jesus family. There is only the family of God, of which we are members. We are inextricably bound not only to Jesus but to all our family. Paul said it over and over in his letters to congregations.

To the Roman church, he said that we are "individually members one of another" (Rom. 12:5). To the Ephesian church, he repeated that "we are members one of another" (Eph. 4:25). To the Corinthian church, he said that "in one Spirit we were all baptized into one body" so now "you are the body of Christ and individually members of it" (1 Cor. 12:13, 27).

There are no solitary Christians, leading independent lives, needing only Jesus but not the church, just as there are no solitary toes or ears or eyes, leading an existence apart from the rest of the human body, needing only a personal relationship with the Creator but not the rest of the body.

Nate Larkin came to understand this the hard way. He was raised in the church. His father was an evangelist and pastor. Nate was the kind of Sunday school kid who always wore his Sunday best and could spout all the Bible memory verses without missing a word. Eventually he would even follow in his father's footsteps and enter the ministry.

He also, over time, would enter the dark world of porn and prostitutes. He was leading a double life that no one knew about. But he kept telling himself that he could break free from this enslavement on his own. He was, after all, "an American male, a rugged individualist by temperament and training."[13] Even when his secret life blew up in his face, when his sins were exposed, he "didn't want help—not *human* help. I wanted God to help me, without involving anybody else."[14]

Nate, after all, had a personal relationship with Jesus. When his double life really bothered him, he'd just double down on that relationship. He'd make vows to get up before the crack of dawn, spend more devotional time with Christ, pray longer prayers, learn more Bible verses by heart. It would seem to work for a few days, but then his life would fall to pieces again. He needed more. He needed something better. As Nate put it, "My personal relationship with Christ hadn't worked, and I knew it was my fault. What I did not yet understand was that while Jesus does offer a personal relationship to every one of his disciples, he never promises any of us a *private* one."[15]

What he needed—what we all need—is the body of Christ. Nate began to realize this. And with that realization, and the growing unity he enjoyed especially with his brothers in Christ, he was able to find in them the kind of relationship he had needed all along: a group relationship. They reminded him that we may all be unique, we may all be snowflakes, but we're "all composed of the same stuff. We all fall to the ground, and we achieve our most captivating beauty in community."[16]

Nate learned the lesson we all need to learn: that failure to cultivate a personal relationship with Jesus is a vital part of being faithful. A privatized faith is a dying faith. We survive and thrive, we grow and flourish, as part of the body of Jesus.

The Us over the Me

Baptist author Jared Wilson writes,

> The American church has done a great disservice in merging one's journey of faith with the values of the American dream. We like to use phrases like "personal Lord and Savior" and "personal relationship with Jesus," neither of which is wrong, per se, but neither do they reflect the fullness of life in Jesus' kingdom. The truth is that while we are saved as individuals, we are not saved to an individual walk. And while our faith may be personal, it is not private.[17]

We are saved not to an individual walk but to a corporate journey in which every step is impossible without others. They need us and we need them. God is a firm believer in community. He created it.

When Jesus taught his disciples how to pray, he told them to address God as "Our Father" (Matt. 6:9). God is certainly my Father. And he is certainly your Father. But in the prayer our Lord gave us, we pray not as isolated individuals but as a family. Our Father in heaven. Our Father who gave us Jesus our brother. Our Father who sent the Spirit into our hearts. Our Father who binds us all together in indissoluble bonds as a church, a community, a body. We never pray alone. We may pray *while* alone, but we never pray alone.

Unheard by us but heard by our Father are a chorus of other voices. Our prayers unite with those of the whole church in heaven and on earth. They enter the ear of Jesus and exit his mouth into the ear of our Father. Our prayers are heard as Jesus's prayers. We are, after all, his body. When the toe prays, when the elbow prays, when the shoulder prays—when all of us who individually make up the body pray—all our prayers go through the mouth of Jesus in a unified petition to the Father of us all.

Even our reading and studying of the Bible is not a solo spiritual exercise. We study the Scriptures communally, even if we're sitting alone in our recliner with the Bible on our lap. The Bible we read—the book itself—is a product of a community. A community made the hard, Spirit-led decisions as to which books were in the canon and which were not, how they were arranged, how they were divided into chapters and verses, and how they were translated. The sacred book we hold in our hands is the result of countless generations of believers. It's a far cry from a personal book we read privately. We also study it, often unconsciously, with the wisdom of parents, Sunday school teachers, pastors, professors, authors, and others guiding us. Our knowledge, assumptions, and beliefs were shaped by them. Just as we pray, "Our Father," so we hold in our hands "our Bible." It's not the book for fostering a personal relationship with Jesus but the book of the church whereby our Lord speaks to us, his bride, communally and corporately—even when we're sitting all alone.

The early church, on the heels of Pentecost, "devoted themselves to the apostles' teaching and the fellowship, to the breaking of bread and the prayers" (Acts 2:42). What's more, "all who believed were together and had all things in common. And they were selling their possessions and belongings and distributing the proceeds to all, as any had need" (vv. 44–45). Day after day they were "attending the temple together and breaking bread in their homes, [and] they received their food with glad and generous hearts, praising God and having favor with all the people. And the Lord added to their number day by day those who were being saved" (vv. 46–47). Notice the corporate life of early believers. They gathered together for worship, study, prayer, meals, and fellowship. They sacrificed their possessions to care for others in the community. They transformed their homes into gathering spaces for their brothers and sisters in Christ. There is not the slightest hint of a Me-centered Christianity. There is, in fact, a complete failure at privatizing the faith. In Acts we see exemplified what Paul meant when he wrote that we are "individually members one of another" (Rom. 12:5).

Paul's words to the first-century Romans are just as much Paul's words to us. In a society intoxicated with the personal, where our world often shrinks to the size of a smartphone screen, where self-this and self-that are all the rage, what believers need is not one more personal thing. Not a personal Bible, not a personal prayer, not a personal Jesus with whom each individual has a personal relationship. Rather, we need a reformation that recovers and celebrates the church. The body of Christ. The family of believers. The Us over the Me.

I was in the middle of writing this chapter when I took a break to lead a men's retreat at Camp Lone Star near La Grange, Texas. About seventy men from various congregations gathered together to spend the weekend in prayer, study of the Word, worship, fellowship, and service projects. The ages spanned from teenagers to old-timers. In between my teaching sessions, I visited with a friend from college whom I hadn't seen in over two decades. I picked the brain of an experienced leader of a congregational men's ministry. I sat around with a group of men to talk about everything from wrestling, to children, to divorce, to hunting.

After our final session together, something unexpected happened. Something I haven't experienced in over twenty-five years. The men gathered around me. These, my brothers, laid their hands upon me. Wrinkled hands, youthful hands, hands with and without wedding rings—they all pressed upon my head, my shoulders, my back. A tangible, physical bond united us. And they prayed for me. They prayed for all of us, for their wives, their families, their churches. I didn't even try to fight back the tears.

I realized, in a new and welcome way, how utterly un-alone I am in the faith. Not only is my life not my own; my faith is not my own either. Ours is a shared faith, a shared hope, a shared love. We are not just metaphorically a body. We are not just symbolically united to each other. We are in truth. When the hands of my brothers, and their prayers, touched me that day, the beauty of our togetherness also touched me.

Jesus didn't establish a community because it seemed like a good idea at the time. He established a community because it is the only good idea for believers. It is for our good. And it is where he gives us his good gifts of forgiveness, life, and salvation.

Blessed are those who fail to have a personal relationship with Jesus but who find their life in the community of believers that is the body of Jesus himself.

9

The Church of St. Big Box

The Failure to Embrace Bigger as Better

would have been lost without Jimmy. And I don't mean metaphorically. I mean I wouldn't have known up from down, left from right. When I parked my car at sunset, put my hard hat on, and walked into the dispatch office to find out which gas wells I was supposed to service that night, the first person I would scout out was Jimmy. He was a living, breathing GPS of the unmapped backcountry where I drove my semi.

Here's how a typical conversation went:

"Hey, Jimmy, you got a minute?"
"Sure, where you heading tonight?"
"Looks like I'm starting off at Cimarex 2119. Where's that?"

"Well, you're gonna go down Quarter Horse Road about three or four miles. When you see a compressor station on your left—it'll be all lit up, you can't miss it—then you take a right across the cattle guard. Follow that road till you see eight white tanks. That's the unit disposal. Veer to your left off the main road onto the ruts. A little ways farther you'll come upon that new well that BP is drilling. Cimarex 2119 will be on the other side of it."

"All right. Thanks. I'll try not to get lost."

"Well, if you do, just look for that BP rig. You can see it for miles."

"Gotcha. Appreciate it."

So it went, night after night, until I had memorized every twist and turn, every barbed wire fence, every well and disposal and rig in that moonlit, rural maze that constituted my vast workspace. Jimmy knew how to give directions. City rules didn't apply. There were no street signs. No exit numbers. Just cows, dirt, and a whole lot of darkness. The only way you're going to get where you're going is by looking for things that stand out. Big things. Bright things. Landmarks that catch the eye.

When giving directions in the country, you go big or you go missing.

What Jimmy did for me is not much different than what most of us do when helping to orient others. For example, when someone asks me where I live, I don't usually say "New Braunfels." I say, "A few miles outside San Antonio." If they ask me where I grew up, I don't say, "Shamrock." I say, "A small town about ninety miles east of Amarillo." As Brad Roth observes in *God's Country*, "We define our geography by cities."[1] Jimmy oriented me by compressor stations, disposals, and rigs because they were the biggest and brightest landmarks in the Texas countryside. When it comes to where we live, we use the nearest city as our landmark. We who live in little places orient others by big places. Size matters.

This all makes perfect sense. It also makes for a perfect parable about another kind of orientation. We often orient our entire lives around a compass that points neither north nor south, neither east nor west. This needle points in only one direction: toward The Big.

What Lurks Beneath?

It's hardly necessary to point out how often size influences our personal, familial, and national decisions. We all want our athletes to win big at the Olympics. We relish a huge stock market uptick. Who doesn't love to receive a hefty raise at work? The fad of "tiny houses" is just that—a fad. Most people are looking to expand, not contract, the square footage of their homes. Even in the most intimate aspects of our lives—our bodies—the focus is on bigger. Case in point: seven times more women receive breast augmentations than breast reductions.[2]

In one or another form or fashion, The Big is always trending in our corporate and individual lives.

Here's the surprise though: The Big is not really about size at all. In fact, ironically, size plays a tiny role in why we assume bigger is better. It's actually not size that matters *but what that size provides us*. We're looking for the fruits of The Big. For instance, we're seeking pride. The bigger our accomplishments, the bigger our pride in what we've done, in who we are, in our self-worth. The bigger our house, the higher we rise in social status. The ultra-rich don't construct mansions because they have thirty overnight guests needing bedrooms. They build them as status symbols. Women have breast augmentations to feel better about their own bodies and/or to appear more attractive to men. It's not size they're going for; it's the result of size. Nations inflate their military not just to have the biggest fighting force on earth. They do it to deter aggression from enemy nations and to ready themselves for potential conflict. There's safety in size.

I can't overemphasize how crucial it is to realize this. Very often The Big seems so irresistible because in it we find something deeper we're searching for. That below-the-surface desire that taps into the longings of our hearts. Once we realize that, we're able to diagnose what gap we're trying to fill with The Big. What foundational human desire are we looking to obtain? Is it pride? Is it self-worth? Security? Status? Acceptance? Trust? Or is it a concoction of all these and possibly more? If we tend to orient our lives around a compass that points toward The Big, then we need to discover what lurks beneath that big house, big job, big savings account, big degree.

As a community of believers, we also need to investigate what lurks beneath the modern phenomenon of another big item: the megachurch. The broadly accepted definition of a megachurch is a congregation that averages two thousand or more people in worship on Sunday. In 2018, the Hartford Institute for Religious Research listed over 1,600 such American churches.[3] The largest of these, Lakewood Church in Houston, where Joel Osteen is pastor, averages 43,500 people on a Sunday. I live in a midsized town in the

Bible Belt with dozens upon dozens of churches, but even we have a megachurch. Such churches average five services per weekend, with considerable variation in worship styles between those services. Most have multiple campuses. Their leaders are often celebrity pastors. And they're a growing phenomenon not only in America but worldwide.[4]

What especially interests me about megachurches could be summed up in a family we'll call the Kirkpatricks. It's Sunday morning in their household. Jim and Leslie, along with their three children, moved into this city from out of state a couple of months ago. They've been looking for a new church home. Jim has talked to a couple of coworkers about area churches, and Leslie has done the same with some moms she met at school. A few names were thrown out there, but one came up repeatedly: Community Bible Church, known by locals simply as CBC. It's associated with the Southern Baptist denomination. What Jim and Leslie hear about CBC is a predictable litany. They hear it's big. It's popular. It's exciting. Since it has services from Saturday night through Sunday afternoon, you can worship at a time that accommodates your schedule and lifestyle. It has cool programs for the kids. It has upbeat music. It has relevant messages. It has a top-notch website. It's inspirational. CBC sounds like a dream church. It has everything the Kirkpatricks are looking for.

So about 9:00 a.m., the family piles into the car and heads northeast toward CBC. It's about a twenty-five-minute drive from their home to the church's campus. Not half a mile from their house, just as they're leaving their neighborhood, they drive past Bethel Baptist Church. There's a few people milling around outside, about thirty or thirty-five cars are in the parking lot, and the service is about to begin. But the Kirkpatricks keep going.

Jim looks down and sees he's running low on gas, so he stops at a convenience store a couple of miles from home. As he's fueling up, he looks directly across the street, where Calvary Baptist is. This congregation has a newly built sanctuary and a detached educational building. Jim tops off the tank, climbs back into the car, and drives on, leaving this congregation behind too. In fact, in the time it takes the Kirkpatricks to cover the distance from their suburban home to CBC, they pass no less than fifty churches that belong to their denomination, and hundreds more from other communions. Some have forty people in worship, others several hundred. They all have songs and sermons and Bible classes. Many have youth programs, VBS, and childcare. But the Kirkpatricks drive by every single one of them. Most don't even register on their radar.

It may be farther, it may be outside their immediate community, it may be in a different school district, it may already have eight thousand other people in attendance, but CBC is where they're going. The needle in the compass of the Kirkpatrick church life points in one direction and one direction only: toward the biggest church around.

The question is, What lurks beneath? If The Big is not really about size at all but rather what that size can get us, what can CBC give the Kirkpatricks? What longings in their hearts do they think this megachurch will satisfy?

For one, supersized congregations like CBC give us options, options give us control, and control satisfies our desire for independence and self-determination. In this way, megachurches are quintessentially American in ethos. We are given a spiritual menu of options: we choose which service, with its distinctive music and worship style, fits our taste; which small group scratches our itch; which service time accommodates our schedule; which preacher we prefer listening to; which men's or women's or youth ministry we might want to get involved in; whether we prefer old-timey black coffee or a Venti salted caramel mocha double blended with extra whipped cream from the church's Jehovah Java booth. We aren't forced to accept a single service time on Sunday, with the same pastor preaching every week, worship patterned after a centuries-old liturgy, and a pot of Folgers brewed by the widowed Mrs. Schmidt. We are empowered to make choices. We exercise our independence. We select what suits our tastes. We are shaping our worship experience every weekend.

Or, to put it differently, we are like spiritual customers shopping for personal preferences at a congregational mall.

The Kirkpatricks also, like most of us, prefer to be identified not with failure but with success. And in our society, nothing trumpets success like big numbers, big buildings, big names, big budgets. We like being on the winning team. At work, our performance is deemed successful if analytics demonstrate that our numbers are up. At school, where we rank on the academic scale is determined by numbers. At church too, how well we're doing is measured numerically. Nobody brags about being part of a shrinking church. But there's great excitement in growth. There's reassurance that we're on the right path, in the right group. There's pride in the need to add more services, build bigger sanctuaries, add more congregational staff, and expand the parking lot a few extra acres.

Nothing says success in modern Christianity more than being the biggest church in town.

And there's one more thing that lurks beneath the Kirkpatricks' desire to attend the local megachurch: it's easier. It's easier to imagine God is at work in a sports-stadium-turned-worship-facility in which fifteen thousand worshipers are amassed than a storefront mission with fifteen people sitting around in folding chairs. It's easier to sense the spiritual excitement in the air with thousands of people around you, a band rocking the place, professional light shows, and even fog machines, than it is with seventy-five people sitting in pews, singing "Amazing Grace" to a piano, and listening to a preacher who's neither young nor hip nor funny nor even that interesting personally.

Megachurches seem to make the kingdom of God see-able, tangible, feelable. The bigger the crowd, the bigger the noise, the bigger the fame, the bigger the professionalism, the bigger the band, the smaller the need there is to see God at work in the mundane, the old, the simple, the unawesome. It's already hard to see God at work in the daily grind of our lives. We don't want that difficulty to bleed over into Sunday as well.

Perhaps I'm being too hard on the Kirkpatricks. I hope so. We're in dire need of hard truths, in-our-face realities that point out how robotically accepting we are of the cultural idolization of size and numbers. We have assumed, almost without question, that bigger is better. It's as if retail giants have become patron saints of the church, as if the superstore model is the superchurch model.

It's time to rethink. To recalibrate our spiritual compasses. It's time to pursue and embrace one more failure: the failure to go big or go home, the failure to idolize numbers, the failure to seek ease and control in size. It's time to rejoice not in megachurches or mini-churches or middle-of-the-road churches—to close our eyes to size. Instead, let's rejoice in churches that have a laser-like focus on one thing and one thing only: determining to know nothing among us except Jesus Christ and him crucified.

Let's follow Joe's example.

A Running Dog with Tin Cans Tied to Its Tail

Jordan Peterson writes, "In a small town, everyone knows who you are. You drag your years behind you like a running dog with tin cans tied to its tail."[5] Joe Jernigan knew this truth painfully well. He was the running dog. And the dozens of tin cans tied to his tail were all labeled Coors and Budweiser and Miller. And in the teetotaling town of Shamrock, Texas, where the sale of alcoholic beverages was prohibited, where Blue Laws were carved onto stone tablets, those cans made a whole lot of racket.

Joe started drinking when most kids start drinking in small towns—as soon as they can get away with it. Shamrock was in a "dry" county, but just about anyone, of any age, could purchase liquor fifteen miles away in the tiny border town of Texola, Oklahoma. And purchase liquor Joe did. Six packs, twelve packs, whole cases. Some kids were weekend drinkers. But Joe was a seven-day-a-week drinker. And his consumption levels kept rising. And as they did, his reputation kept lowering. Locals referred to him with contempt as "that Jernigan boy." As in, "There goes that Jernigan boy again, heading to Texola." Or,

"That Jernigan boy is turning into a hellion." Or, "That Jernigan boy is gonna drink himself into an early grave." The tin cans tied to his tail kept multiplying. And so did their noise.

Joe eventually packed his bags and moved away. But he took his alcoholism with him. And its brood of shame and guilt and self-destruction. Over time, beaten and bottomed out, having nearly drunk his liver into an early grave, like the prodigal son he came crawling back home. Only the person running out to meet him was not his father but his mother. She saved his life, literally. She loved him, forgave him, and got him into rehab. Joe got sober. He got better. Christ too got hold of him. Loved him. Forgave him. Saved him. That Jernigan boy became the Father's child.

This all happened about forty-five years ago. Today, on the south side of this small town, on Main Street, there is a congregation called Calvary Christian Fellowship. And every Sunday, standing up front, is a smiling, jovial, seventysomething preacher whom every citizen of Shamrock knows as Brother Joe.

That Jernigan boy came back to his hometown. He came back to where everyone knew his sin so that he might tell everyone about his Savior. He came back to the parking lots where he had downed beer after beer to preach about the sober intoxication of the Spirit. And over time, those tin cans tied to his tail were drowned out by the Amens sounding from those who heard him preach.

He started small. Found a little building that he transformed into a little church, with a little flock of people and very little money. But he had a big message. He had the biggest message of the world to preach, to teach, to share house to house, person to person, over and over again. It was the message of a God who doesn't give up on people, even when others do, even when—perhaps especially when—they give up on themselves. Joe, who had sinned much and been forgiven much, loved much. And that love has shown in and out of church. It shows in his preaching, his care of souls, his compassion and his zeal to bring sinners into the kingdom of grace.

Brother Joe never set out to start a megachurch. He set out to preach Jesus. To keep his feet firmly planted on the soil beneath the cross. There's a reason the congregation he's pastored all these years is named Calvary. It's a group of forgiven sinners washed in the blood of the Lamb whose life was sacrificed on Calvary's altar. The congregation is often home to locals who don't feel like they're "good enough" or "spiritual enough" or "have a clean enough past" to fit into other local churches. They too are like dogs with tin cans tied to their tails. But Brother Joe and Calvary welcome them, love them, forgive them, baptize them, and embrace them as brothers and sisters of the same heavenly Father.

That Jernigan boy turned Christian, turned pastor, turned church planter, has spent his entire ministry in Shamrock. He and his wife, D'Anna, have impacted the lives of thousands over the years through their work at Calvary. Thousands? Or is it tens of thousands? Or more? Who really cares? They're not counting. If the angels of God rejoice over one sinner who repents, then how can the church withhold its applause until we get to ten or one hundred or one thousand or more? What matters is not the size of the audience but the fidelity of the message. And that message for Joe has always been the same: Christ crucified and risen for us.

Brother Joe has been a failure in the best possible way: he's failed to build a foundation other than that already laid—the foundation of Jesus's blood and righteousness. On that foundation Calvary Christian Fellowship is built. On that foundation every church worthy of the name is built, no matter how big or small its edifice might be.

A Successful Church Is above Our Pay Grade

We have metrics to show when a business is successful. We can look at its bottom line, its productivity, its popularity with customers. We can crunch the numbers. They will give us an objective answer. A growing company is usually a successful company. Evidently, as we've learned in recent years, a company can even become "too big to fail." Imagine that.

We have no metrics, however, to show when a church is successful. I mean zero. A congregation with ten thousand people may or may not be more successful than a congregation of ten. A congregation of ten may or may not be more successful than a congregation of ten thousand. We have no way to know. We can't determine success based on attendance, offering, surveys, retention of staff, or the number of new visitors or returning worshipers. As Tim Suttle says, "Success is the kind of metric we simply don't know how to handle. It's above our pay grade."[6]

There have been seasons in the church's history when it seemed to prosper and seasons when it seemed to decline. Way back in Elijah's day he pouted to God that he was the sole survivor of the worshipers of Yahweh. He was wrong, of course, as God pointed out. There were actually seven thousand who hadn't bowed the knee to Baal (1 Kings 19:14, 18). During the dark days of the Soviet Union, when pastors and priests were systematically executed or shipped off to Siberia, when millions of believers were martyred by the totalitarian state, it must have seemed to many Russian Christians as if the church would perish, never to return. But it didn't perish. And it's flourishing today. As G. K. Chesterton once quipped, "Christianity has died many times and risen again; for it had a God who knew the way out of the grave."[7]

Christianity also has a God who knows that if the church runs the way of success, we'll eventually tumble headfirst into the grave of irrelevance. That's where the quest for success leads us—into a kind of death, into a toothless message of empty platitudes with a mirage of hope at the end.

Our churches, in fact, preach a kind of unsuccess. We succeed at nothing to which the world aspires. Power? No, we boast in weakness. Fame? No, we revel in anonymity. Beauty? No, our God hung on an ugly cross. Winning? No, we confess that the first are actually last. Riches? No, for the love of them is the root of all kinds of evil. The church is a place for losers. For those whose hands have been emptied, so that—as we sing—"nothing in my hand I bring, simply to the cross I cling."[8]

Simply to the cross we cling. And simply to the cross we direct sinners. Or, to put it more precisely, we bring the cross to sinners. Every sermon is like a basket full of life-giving fruit picked from the cross tree and passed out to everyone who hungers for grace. Every hymn and song is like a pitcher of water, filled from the fountain of the cross, taken to those fevered by evil, to slake their thirst. Every Lord's Supper is a feast of the Lamb of God, which brings the food of the cross to starving sinners that they might taste and see that the Lord is good.

The church doesn't take people back to the cross but takes the cross to where people are now. On mountaintops of laughter or vales of tears. Happily married or shattered by divorce. Free or incarcerated. Moral or immoral. One day or a hundred years old. We determine to know one thing and one thing only: Jesus is the answer to every human hurt, every human failure, every human shame, every human desire. He and he alone is what the church has to offer: a crucified God for a dying humanity, a risen God who breathes life back into the world, a reigning God who wields power over creation by loving us into a state of re-creation.

A church driven by the desire for the world's version of success can never preach that. It won't sell. It's not nearly sexy enough. It will, in fact, drive many away, as Jesus himself experienced when many of his followers couldn't stomach his "hard saying" (John 6:60). But the church can shrug at all that. It's not our concern. We simply hand out what Jesus has given us. Like the sower in Jesus's parable who acts like a blind farmer, throwing the seed willy-nilly—on rocks, across footpaths, by weeds, and on good soil—so the church throws the gospel around. Liberally. Haphazardly. Without a thought for whether the person has a heart like asphalt or potting soil. That's not our responsibility. We're not in the business of choosing the right kind of people to preach to. Success is not our motivation. Fidelity is. Being faithful to grab handfuls of Jesus and cast them into the wind to see where the Spirit might carry them—that's our task.

To make disciples of all nations by baptizing them in the name of the Father and of the Son and of the Holy Spirit, and by teaching them to observe all that Christ has commanded us (Matt. 28:19–20). Not to make people Republicans or Democrats, not to make them rich or poor, not even to make them Baptists or Lutherans or Catholics or Presbyterians, but to make them children of the Father, heirs of the Spirit, siblings of our elder brother, Jesus.

To put it crassly, when it comes to numbers, the church's give-a-damn ought to be broken. Are there ten in the service this morning? Good! Are there a thousand? Good! Did fifty people quit the church last week because they got sick and tired of hearing about Jesus, Jesus, Jesus all the time? Good! They were evidently here for something other than church anyway. Did fifty more come in to replace them? Good!

You know what's even better? To quit counting. To cease and desist from metrics and analytics and graphs and chest-thumping over numerical growth.

If we're going to get excited over something, can it please be the gospel? Can we jump up and down over pastors who can't wait to preach about what Jesus did for us? Can we stop worrying about how skilled our pastors are at fundraising and life-coaching and marriage counseling and, instead, make sure that when they step into the pulpit, we're going to hear about the God who loves us and saves us in Jesus Christ?

When it comes to The Big in Christianity, let's all be big-time failures. Failing to care about how mega or mini our churches are. Failing to care about how many churches are closing their doors and how many are just opening up. Failing to care about dying denominations or newly arrived communities. That's all a numbers game. And a game the church has not been called to play. We don't know the rules.

What we do know is this: Jesus told us to go "into all the world and proclaim the gospel to the whole creation" (Mark 16:15). He never said to send back annual reports. He never told us how big the optimal congregation is. He simply said to preach the Good News. When the church does that, the heavenly host break out in song, the Father's smile stretches from ear to ear, the Spirit soars on the wings of joy, and the Son opens his arms to take in a world of laboring and heavy-laden sinners who find rest in him.

Blessed are those who fail to believe that bigger is better and who discover contentment and joy in the little message that floods the whole world with peace: Jesus Christ, crucified and risen, for us.

Epilogue

We began our journey together through these chapters with a handwritten note inside a used book that asked, "Does it matter what one believes? Or is anything okay, just so long as you feel good about it?" What we've discovered, along the way, is that all of God's truths matter, but they don't necessarily make us feel good. Often they make us uncomfortable because they're so counterintuitive to what we hear shouted in society and whispered in our own hearts. When our Father opens his mouth, chances are what comes out won't at first make sense to us. Indeed, it may never make sense to us. But it will make us new. It will remake our minds and hearts. His backward, unexpected words will turn our lives inside out. They will produce the exact kind of shake-up we need to reorient our hearts so that we're ready to hear and believe and do God's will.

That will is always the will of a loving Father. What he wants for us—his will for us—is to plant us so deeply within his Son that we bear his image, echo his speech, and walk in his ways. Our lives are hidden with Christ in God, and they are revealed with Christ in this world. They are revealed in varieties of blessedness that characterize us as individuals, workers and families, and worshipers. They are beatitudes that look ugly and weird in the eyes of the world but sparkle with perfect beauty in the eyes of our Father. And isn't that all that matters?

All that matters is that God is pleased with us in Christ, that Christ lives and moves within us, and that the Spirit turns our lives upside down so that our spirituality is now right side up from heaven's perspective.

May our gracious God—Father, Son, and Holy Spirit—plant these beatitudes within us so that they grow and flourish, we live in newness of life, and the church is rightly accused of turning the world upside down.

The Beatitudes of Upside-Down Spirituality

> Blessed are those who fail to believe in themselves, who fail to believe that God believes in them, for they shall find in Jesus-only everything their heart desires.

> Blessed are those who don't make a name for themselves but rejoice that their names are written in the Lamb's book of life.

> Blessed are those who don't follow their hearts, for they follow the Lamb wherever he goes.

> Blessed are those who fail at being supermoms and superdads, for they are forgiven children of our Father in heaven.

Blessed are those who fail to find their calling, for theirs is the kingdom where life and love and service find them.

Blessed are those who fail at finding anyone in this world who completes them and who fail at sustaining their marriages by love alone but are completed and perfected in Christ, and whose marriages are sustained by the gift of Jesus and his limitless love.

Blessed are those who fail to conform to this world yet also fail to cut themselves off from it, for they know their true citizenship is in Jerusalem above.

Blessed are those who fail to have a personal relationship with Jesus but who find their life in the community of believers that is the body of Jesus himself.

Blessed are those who fail to believe that bigger is better and who discover contentment and joy in the little message that floods the whole world with peace: Jesus Christ, crucified and risen, for us.

Notes

Introduction

1. For the original sources of these quotes and a thorough discussion of these accusations, see chap. 1 of Larry Hurtado, *Destroyer of the Gods: Early Christian Distinctiveness in the Roman World* (Waco, TX: Baylor University Press, 2016).

2. C. S. Lewis, *Mere Christianity* (New York: MacMillan, 1952), 174.

3. Michael May, "Total Failure: How George Foreman's Losses Showed Him the Light," *All Things Considered*, May 24, 2017, http://www.npr.org/2017/05/24/528995768/total-failure-how-george-foremans-losses-showed-him-the-light. All quotes are from this article.

Chapter 1 The Good News That God Doesn't Believe in You

1. This quote is often attributed to Ralph Waldo Emerson or Oliver Wendell Holmes, but probably originated with Henry Stanley Haskins. See http://quoteinvestigator.com/2011/01/11/what-lies-within/.

2. Attributed to Brad Henry. See, for example, Danielle, "Brad Henry, Founder," *Gather and Lounge*, June 8, 2015, http://gatherandlounge.com/brad-henry-founder/.

3. A variety of versions exist for this prayer, traditionally ascribed to St. Patrick (mid-fifth century). This one is taken from http://www.ourcatholicprayers.com/st-patricks-breastplate.html.

4. Ludaemilia Elisabeth, "Jesus, Jesus, Only Jesus," 1687, trans. August Crull (1880). Public domain. For the full text, see http://www.lutheran-hymnal.com/lyrics/tlh348.htm.

5. Bo Giertz, *The Hammer of God*, trans. Clifford A. Nelson (Minneapolis, MN: Augsburg Publishing House, 1973). *The Hammer of God* is a collection of three novellas, each of which tells the story of a pastor who struggles to come to grips with the all-sufficient grace of God. Fridfeldt's story is the second of these.

6. Paul Zahl describes these little-l laws this way: "The principle of divine demand for perfection upon the human being is reflected concretely in the countless internal and external demands that human beings devise for themselves. In practice, the requirement of perfect submission to the commandments of God is exactly the same as the requirement of perfect submission to the innumerable drives for perfection that drive everyday people's crippled and crippling lives." Paul Zahl, *Grace in Practice: A Theology of Everyday Life* (Grand Rapids: Eerdmans, 2007), 28.

7. William McDavid, Ethan Richardson, and David Zahl, *Law and Gospel: A Theology for Sinners (and Saints)* (Charlottesville, VA: Mockingbird Ministries, 2015), 18.

8. Giertz, *Hammer of God*, 203–4.

9. Giertz, *Hammer of God*, 204.

10. Robert F. Capon, *The Mystery of Christ (and Why We Don't Get It)* (Grand Rapids: Eerdmans, 1993), 21.

11. Capon, *The Mystery of Christ*, 90–91.

Chapter 2 What If I Just Want to Be Average?

1. Brooks and Dunn, "Only in America," *Steers & Stripes* (Arista Nashville, 2001).

2. As quoted in Jenna Krajeski, "This Is Water," *New Yorker*, September 19, 2008, http://www.newyorker.com/books/page-turner/this -is-water.

3. He writes, "So we see that sin is and acts the same everywhere. It does not want to be sin; it does not want to be punished because of sin. It wants to be righteousness." Martin Luther, *Lectures on Genesis: Chapters 1–5*, vol. 1 of *Luther's Works*, American ed. (St. Louis: Concordia Publishing House, 1958), 179.

4. For a thorough discussion of ambition's rise from vice to virtue, see Michael Horton, *Ordinary: Sustainable Faith in a Radical, Restless World* (Grand Rapids: Zondervan, 2014), 87–103.

5. Brennan Manning, *Abba's Child: The Cry of the Heart for Intimate Belonging* (Colorado Springs: NavPress, 2015), 73. Manning's quote is from John Shea, *Starlight: Beholding the Christmas Miracle All Year Long* (New York: Crossroad, 1993), 92.

6. Bo Giertz, *With My Own Eyes*, trans. Bror Erickson (Irvine, CA: NRP Books/New Reformation Publications), 155.

7. Giertz, *With My Own Eyes*, 155.

8. Horton, *Ordinary*, 88.

9. Quoted by James Finley, *Merton's Palace of Nowhere: A Search for God through Awareness of the True Self* (Notre Dame, IN: Ave Maria Press, 1978), 54.

Chapter 3 Go Home, Heart, You're Drunk

1. R. Laird Harris, ed., *Theological Wordbook of the Old Testament*, vol. 1 (Chicago: Moody Press, 1980), 466.

2. James K. A. Smith, *You Are What You Love: The Spiritual Power of Habit* (Grand Rapids: Brazos, 2016), 8.

3. Smith, *You Are What You Love*, 1.

4. Marie Kondo, *The Life-Changing Magic of Tidying Up: The Japanese Art of Decluttering and Organizing* (New York: Random House, 2014).

5. Taffy Brodesser-Akner, "Marie Kondo and the Ruthless War on Stuff," *New York Times*, July 6, 2016, https://www.nytimes.com/2016/07/10/magazine/marie-kondo-and-the-ruthless-war-on-stuff.html.

6. A line from Alanis Morissette's hit single "Ironic," *Jagged Little Pill* (Maverick, 1995).

7. G. K. Chesterton, *Orthodoxy* (San Francisco: Ignatius Press, 1995), 102.

8. Smith, *You Are What You Love*, 1.

9. Kimm Crandall, *Beloved Mess: God's Perfect Love for Your Imperfect Life* (Grand Rapids: Baker, 2016).

Chapter 4 Supermoms, Über Dads, and Other People Who Don't Exist

1. Miranda Lambert, "The House That Built Me," *Revolution* (Columbia Nashville, 2010).

2. William Makepeace Thackeray, *Vanity Fair*, serialized in *Punch* (1847–1848), chap. 51.

3. "Be a Fun Mum" Facebook timeline post, May 5, 2017, https://www.facebook.com/Be.A.Fun.Mum/photos/a.131934583910.106221.122111748910/10155203352798911/?type=3&theater.

4. "ABQ," *Breaking Bad*, season 2, episode 13, directed by Adam Bernstein, written by Vince Gilligan, aired May 31, 2009, on AMC.

5. "Phoenix," *Breaking Bad*, season 2, episode 12, directed by Colin Bucksey, written by John Shiban, aired May 24, 2009, on AMC.

6. Chesterton, *Orthodoxy*, 81.

7. Chesterton, *Orthodoxy*, 81.

8. William Martin, "Make the Ordinary Come Alive," *The Parent's Tao Te Ching: Ancient Advice for Modern Parents* (Boston: Da Capo Press, 2009), 35.

9. Elyse Fitzpatrick and Jessica Thompson, *Give Them Grace: Dazzling Your Kids with the Love of Jesus* (Wheaton, IL: Crossway, 2011), 164.

10. Fitzpatrick and Thompson, *Give Them Grace*, 21.

11. Brené Brown, *The Gifts of Imperfection: Let Go of Who You Think You're Supposed to Be and Embrace Who You Are* (Center City, MN: Hazelden Publishing, 2010), 56.

Chapter 5 My Altar Has a Diesel Engine

1. John Barnett, "Seek First His Kingdom: An Invitation to Christian Vocation," *Christ at Work: Orthodox Christian Perspectives on Vocation* (Brookline, MA: Holy Cross Orthodox Press, 2006), 43.

2. Barnett, "Seek First His Kingdom," 59.

3. "Church Staff Learns Fresh Batch of Buzzwords That Will Be Meaningless in Six Months," *Babylon Bee*, May 12, 2017, http://babylon bee.com/news/church-staff-learns-fresh-batch-buzzwords-will-meaning less-six-months/.

4. Martin Luther, "The Freedom of a Christian," *Career of the Reformer I*, vol. 31 of *Luther's Works*, American ed. (Philadelphia: Fortress Press, 1957), 344.

5. Norman Nagel, "Luther and the Priesthood of All Believers," *Concordia Theological Quarterly* (October 1997), 280.

Chapter 6 Love Will Not Sustain Your Marriage

1. He writes, "As high as God is above man, so high are the sanctity, the rights, and the promise of marriage above the sanctity, the rights, and the promise of love. It is not your love that sustains the marriage, but from now on, the marriage that sustains your love." Dietrich Bonhoeffer, "A Wedding Sermon from a Prison Cell," *Letters and Papers from Prison* (New York: Touchstone, 1997), 46.

2. Aziz Ansari and Eric Klinenberg, *Modern Romance* (New York: Penguin, 2015), 214.

3. Ansari and Klinenberg, *Modern Romance*, 214.

4. Ansari and Klinenberg, *Modern Romance*, 214.

5. Ansari and Klinenberg, *Modern Romance*, 215.

6. Ansari and Klinenberg, *Modern Romance*, 215.

7. Ansari relates the advice of psychologist Jonathan Haidt, who urges that we adopt a "narrative view" of marriage, in which the "best life is about building a story" together. Ansari and Klinenberg, *Modern Romance*, 221.

8. Robert F. Capon, *Bed and Board: Plain Talk about Marriage* (New York: Mockingbird Ministries, 2017), 147.

9. Alain de Botton, "Why You Will Marry the Wrong Person," *New York Times*, May 28, 2016.

10. Capon, *Bed and Board*, 40.

11. C. S. Lewis, "The Sermon and the Lunch," *God in the Dock* (New York: HarperOne, 2014), 284.

12. Lewis, "The Sermon and the Lunch," 285.

13. De Botton, "Why You Will Marry the Wrong Person."

14. Gustaf Wingren, *Luther on Vocation*, trans. Carl C. Rasmussen (Evansville, IN: Ballast Press, 1994), 6.

15. Esther Perel, "The Secret to Desire in a Long-Term Relationship," TED Talk, February 2013, https://www.ted.com/talks/esther_perel_the _secret_to_desire_in_a_long_term_relationship/up-next.

Chapter 7 Building Walls and Digging Moats?

1. Kristine Phillips and Sarah Pulliam Bailey, "'Evil Has Invaded Sanctuary': Texas Massacre Likely the Worst Church Shooting in U.S. History," *Washington Post*, November 6, 2017, https://www.washingtonpost .com/news/acts-of-faith/wp/2017/11/06/evil-has-invaded-sanctuary -texas-massacre-likely-the-worst-church-shooting-in-u-s-history/?utm _term=.c287bdbc39f3.

2. Rod Dreher, *The Benedict Option: A Strategy for Christians in a Post-Christian Nation* (New York: Penguin, 2017).

3. Dreher, *Benedict Option*, 155.

4. Dreher, *Benedict Option*, 182.

5. Dreher, *Benedict Option*, 188.

6. Dreher, *Benedict Option*, 12.

7. Even after Cyrus, the Persian king, issued a decree in 538 BC that allowed the Jews to return to their homeland, only a minority did. "After all, Palestine was a faraway land which only the oldest could remember, and the journey thither difficult and dangerous; the future of the venture was at best uncertain. Moreover, many Jews were by this time well established in Babylon." John Bright, *A History of Israel*, third ed. (Philadelphia: Westminster Press, 1981), 362. Indeed, over time, Babylon, not Israel, would become one of the chief centers of Jewish religious studies. The Talmud, for instance, that foundational compendium of Jewish

learning, is the *Babylonian* Talmud. Although a Palestinian version exists, its significance is greatly overshadowed by its Babylonian counterpart.

8. Michael W. Holmes, *The Apostolic Fathers in English* (Grand Rapids: Baker Academic, 2006), 295.

9. Holmes, *Apostolic Fathers in English*, 295–96.

10. James K. A. Smith, *Awaiting the King: Reforming Public Theology* (Grand Rapids: Baker Academic, 2017), 195.

11. A favorite image of James K. A. Smith, who argues that we have reduced people to thinking creatures: "We imagine human beings as giant bobblehead dolls: with humungous heads and itty-bitty, unimportant bodies. . . . 'You are what you think' is a motto that reduces human beings to brains-on-a-stick." *You Are What You Love: The Spiritual Power of Habit* (Grand Rapids: Brazos, 2016), 3.

12. David Zahl, "Here We Still Stand Conference," October 20, 2017 (San Diego, CA), https://www.herewestillstand.org/videos/.

Chapter 8 There's No Such Thing as a Personal Relationship with Jesus

1. Matt Mauney, "History of Asbestos," Asbestos.com, accessed July 31, 2018, https://www.asbestos.com/asbestos/history/.

2. Matt Mauney, "Asbestos Fireproofing and Fire Prevention Materials," Asbestos.com, accessed July 31, 2018, https://www.asbestos.com/products/general/fireproofing-fire-prevention-materials.php.

3. Andrea Boggio, *Compensating Asbestos Victims: Law and the Dark Side of Industrialization* (New York: Routledge, 2016), 155.

4. Mauney, "History of Asbestos."

5. Tom Wolfe, "The 'Me' Decade and the Third Great Awakening," *New York*, August 23, 1976.

6. Wolfe, "The 'Me' Decade."

7. Wolfe, "The 'Me' Decade." Italics added.

8. Stephen Freeman, "Psychology as the New Sacrament," *Glory to God for All Things*, September 13, 2016, https://blogs.ancientfaith.com/glory2godforallthings/2016/09/13/psychology-new-sacrament/comment-page-2/.

9. I am indebted to Joel Miller for this insight, as well as for pointing me to the article by Tom Wolfe. See his blog post, "Why You Need More Than a Personal Relationship with Jesus," *Joel J. Miller's Essays & Commonplaces*, accessed July 31, 2018, https://joeljmiller.com/personal-relationship-jesus/.

10. Depeche Mode, "Personal Jesus," *Violator* (Mute Records, 1990).

11. Charles Austin Miles, "In the Garden," 1913. Public domain.

12. Cyprian of Carthage, "On the Unity of the Church," *Ante-Nicene Fathers* vol. 5 (Peabody, MA: Hendrickson, 1994), 423.

13. Nate Larkin, *Samson and the Pirate Monks: Calling Men to Authentic Brotherhood* (Nashville: Thomas Nelson, 2007), 72.

14. Larkin, *Samson and the Pirate Monks*, 72.

15. Larkin, *Samson and the Pirate Monks*, 73. Italics in original.

16. Larkin, *Samson and the Pirate Monks*, 83.

17. Jared Wilson, *Supernatural Power for Everyday People: Experiencing God's Extraordinary Spirit in Your Ordinary Life* (Nashville: Thomas Nelson, 2018), 136.

Chapter 9 The Church of St. Big Box

1. Brad Roth, *God's Country: Faith, Hope, and the Future of the Rural Church* (Harrisonburg, VA: Herald Press, 2017), 38.

2. ASPS National Clearinghouse of Plastic Surgery Procedural Statistics, "Plastic Surgery Statistics Report 2016," Plasticsurgery.org, accessed August 1, 2018, https://www.plasticsurgery.org/documents/News/Statistics /2016/plastic-surgery-statistics-full-report-2016.pdf.

3. Hartford Seminary, "Database of Megachurches in the U.S.," Hartford Institute for Religion Research, accessed August 1, 2018, http://hirr .hartsem.edu/megachurch/database.html.

4. Scott Thumma and Warren Bird, "Recent Shifts in America's Largest Protestant Churches: Megachurches 2015 Report," Leadership Network and Hartford Institute for Religion Research, accessed August 1, 2018, http://hirr.hartsem.edu/megachurch/2015_Megachurches_Report.pdf.

5. Jordan Peterson, *12 Rules for Life: An Antidote to Chaos* (Toronto: Random House Canada, 2018), 72.

6. Tim Suttle, *Shrink: Faithful Ministry in a Church-Growth Culture* (Grand Rapids: Zondervan, 2014), 41.

7. G. K. Chesterton, *The Everlasting Man* (Brooklyn: Angelico Press, 2013), 216.

8. Augustus M. Toplady, "Rock of Ages, Cleft for Me," stanza 3, 1776. Public domain.

Chad Bird has served as a pastor in the Lutheran Church—Missouri Synod, as an assistant professor of Hebrew and exegetical theology at Concordia Theological Seminary in Fort Wayne, Indiana, and as a guest lecturer at Lutheran Theological Seminary in Novosibirsk, Siberia. He is the author of several books, including *Your God Is Too Glorious*, and has contributed articles to *The Lutheran Witness*, *Gottesdienst*, *Gospel Coalition*, *Concordia Theological Quarterly*, *Modern Reformation*, *Mockingbird*, *Logia*, *Higher Things*, and *The Federalist*. In addition to hosting chadbird.com, he is a regular contributor to christholdfast.org and 1517legacy .com. He lives in Texas.

CONNECT WITH

designed by Brenton Clarke Little

photo credit: Doug Klembara

www.ChadBird.com

Chad Bird   BirdChadLouis   Chad Bird

Listen to **40 Minutes in the Old Testament** on iTunes